Essential VOCA with Stories

1

Essential VOCA with Stories **1**

Written by Michael A. Putlack • Elizabeth Lee

First Published August 2020

Publisher: Kyudo Chung
Editors: Ziin Zong
Designers: Miju Yoon, Miyoung Lim
Photo Credit: www.shutterstock.com

Published and distributed by Happy House, an imprint of DARAKWON
Darakwon Bldg., 211 Moonbal-ro, Paju-si Gyeonggi-do, Korea 10881
Tel: 82-2-736-2031(Ext. 250) Fax: 82-2-732-2037 Homepage: www.ihappyhouse.co.kr

ISBN: 978-89-6653-573-6 63740
Age Range: 12 years and up
Price: ₩14,000

Components
Student Book

Free Downloadable Resources at www.ihappyhouse.co.kr
Answer Key & Translation • MP3 Files • Audio Script • Word List • Word Test

Essential VOCA with Stories

1

Happy House

Table of Contents

How to Use This Book

Target Words

This section contains 20 target words. Comprehensive information about each word is provided. This includes the part of speech, one or more definitions, and one or more expressions that contain the word. There is also one or more sample sentence using the word, so readers can see how to use the word properly.

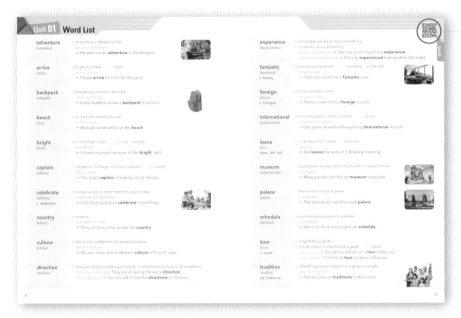

QR cord

Readers can use the QR code to listen to audio recordings of the words and examples sentences.

Unit Exercises

There are a wide variety of exercises for readers to practice the words they learn in Word List. The exercises give readers the opportunity to test their knowledge of the definitions of the words and how the words are used in sentences. There is also a short reading passage containing target words from the unit. Following it are 4 comprehension questions to make sure that readers understand the passage.

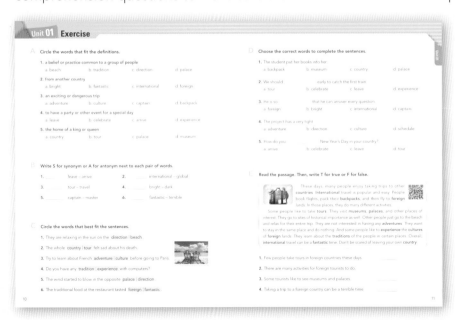

Review Units

After every five units, there is a review unit. This section retests readers on the knowledge they learned in the previous units. There are exercises that test readers on definitions and word usage. Each review unit also contains a crossword puzzle and a reading passage containing target words. Readers must then answer comprehension questions testing their understanding of the passage.

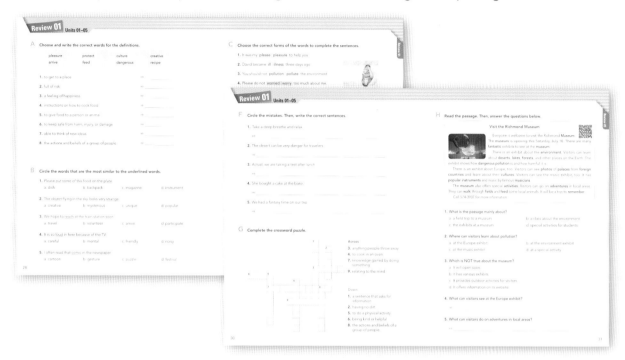

Index

The index contains all of the words in each unit. Readers can use it to search for words while studying.

Answer Key & Translation

The answer key and Korean translation may be downloaded for free at www.ihappyhouse.co.kr.

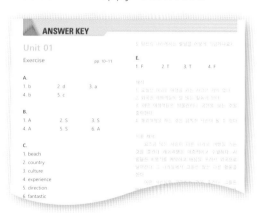

1	**adventure** [ədvéntʃər]	*n.* an exciting or dangerous trip go on an adventure → He went on an **adventure** in the Amazon.

2	**arrive** [əráiv]	*v.* to get to a place (syn) reach arrive on time → Please **arrive** on time for the party.

3	**backpack** [bǽkpæk]	*n.* a large bag carried on the back carry a backpack → Every student carries a **backpack** to school.

4	**beach** [biːtʃ]	*n.* an area with sand by the sea on the beach → We built sandcastles on the **beach**.

5	**bright** [brait]	*adj.* full of light; smart (syn) sunny (ant) dark bright light → I closed my eyes because of the **bright** light.

6	**captain** [kǽptin]	*n.* the person in charge of a ship or airplane (syn) master ship's captain → The ship's **captain** is looking out at the sea.

7	**celebrate** [sélibrèit] *n.* celebration	*v.* to have a party or other event for a special day celebrate one's birthday → Let's have a party to **celebrate** his birthday.

8	**country** [kántri]	*n.* a nation across the country → They went on a trip across the **country**.

9	**culture** [káltʃər]	*n.* the actions and beliefs of a group of people Western culture → We also learn about Western **culture** in English class.

10	**direction** [dirékʃən]	*n.* the point where something is moving; *pl.* information on how to do something the same direction → They are all going the same **direction**. follow directions → You should follow the **directions** on the box.

11 **experience**
[ikspí(:)əriəns]

n. knowledge gained by doing something

v. to learn by doing something

teaching experience → She has a lot of teaching **experience**.

experience bad weather → The city **experienced** bad weather last night.

12 **fantastic**
[fæntǽstik]

n. fantasy

adj. amazing; impressive [syn] wonderful [ant] terrible

fantastic view

→ The hotel room has a **fantastic** view.

13 **foreign**
[fɔ́:rən]

n. foreigner

adj. from another country

foreign country

→ Pedro comes from a **foreign** country.

14 **international**
[ìntərnǽʃənəl]

adj. involving two or more countries [syn] global

international airport

→ Our plane arrived at Hong Kong **International** Airport.

15 **leave**
[li:v]
leave - left - left

v. to go away from a place [ant] arrive

leave for

→ She **leaves** for work at 7:30 every morning.

16 **museum**
[mju(:)zí(:)əm]

n. a place that displays items of historical or cultural interest

art museum

→ Many people visit the art **museum** every year.

17 **palace**
[pǽləs]

n. the home of a king or queen

royal palace

→ The tourists will visit the royal **palace**.

18 **schedule**
[skédʒu:l]

n. a plan showing a person's activities

on schedule

→ We must finish our project on **schedule**.

19 **tour**
[tuər]

n. tourist

n. a trip led by a guide

v. to visit a place of interest with a guide [syn] travel

go on a tour → Our family will go on a **tour** of Beijing.

tour a palace → I'd like to **tour** a palace in Europe.

20 **tradition**
[trədíʃən]

adj. traditional

n. a belief or practice common to a group of people

pass on a tradition

→ Fathers pass on **traditions** to their sons.

A   Circle the words that fit the definitions.

1. a belief or practice common to a group of people

   a. beach   b. tradition   c. direction   d. palace

2. from another country

   a. bright   b. fantastic   c. international   d. foreign

3. an exciting or dangerous trip

   a. adventure   b. culture   c. captain   d. backpack

4. to have a party or other event for a special day

   a. leave   b. celebrate   c. arrive   d. experience

5. the home of a king or queen

   a. country   b. tour   c. palace   d. museum

B   Write S for synonym or A for antonym next to each pair of words.

1. _____ leave – arrive   **2.** _____ international – global

3. _____ tour – travel   **4.** _____ bright – dark

5. _____ captain – master   **6.** _____ fantastic – terrible

C   Circle the words that best fit the sentences.

1. They are relaxing in the sun on the   direction | beach .

2. The whole   country | tour   felt sad about his death.

3. Try to learn about French   adventure | culture   before going to Paris.

4. Do you have any   tradition | experience   with computers?

5. The wind started to blow in the opposite   palace | direction .

6. The traditional food at the restaurant tasted   foreign | fantastic .

D Choose the correct words to complete the sentences.

1. The student put her books into her _____.

    a. backpack   b. museum   c. country   d. palace

2. We should _____ early to catch the first train.

    a. tour   b. celebrate   c. leave   d. experience

3. He is so _____ that he can answer every question.

    a. foreign   b. bright   c. international   d. captain

4. The project has a very tight _____.

    a. adventure   b. direction   c. culture   d. schedule

5. How do you _____ New Year's Day in your country?

    a. arrive   b. celebrate   c. leave   d. tour

E Read the passage. Then, write T for true or F for false.

These days, many people enjoy taking trips to other countries. **International** travel is popular and easy. People book flights, pack their **backpacks**, and then fly to **foreign** lands. In those places, they do many different activities.

Some people like to take **tours**. They visit **museums**, **palaces**, and other places of interest. They go to sites of historical importance as well. Other people just go to the beach and relax for their entire trip. They are not interested in having any **adventures**. They want to stay in the same place and do nothing. And some people like to **experience** the **cultures** of **foreign** lands. They learn about the **traditions** of the people in certain places. Overall, **international** travel can be a **fantastic** time. Don't be scared of leaving your own **country**.

1. Few people take tours in foreign countries these days. _____

2. There are many activities for foreign tourists to do. _____

3. Some tourists like to see museums and palaces. _____

4. Taking a trip to a foreign country can be a terrible time. _____

1

act
[ækt]
n. action

v. to do something; to play in a movie, musical, etc.
act quickly
→ The firefighters **acted** quickly to put out the fire.

2

bake
[beik]
n. bakery

v. to cook in an oven
bake a cake
→ I will **bake** a cake for her birthday.

3

cage
[keidʒ]

n. a box in which people keep animals
lion cage
→ The lion **cage** has strong bars.

4

cartoon
[kɑːrtúːn]

n. a funny drawing in a newspaper; a children's movie or TV program with moving pictures   (syn) comic
cartoon character
→ Mickey Mouse is a famous **cartoon** character.

5

collect
[kəlékt]
n. collection

v. to gather items that are similar; to bring together
collect coins
→ Jenny **collects** coins as a hobby.

6

costume
[kástjuːm]

n. special clothes people wear at events
Halloween costume
→ What is your Halloween **costume** this year?

7

exercise
[éksərsàiz]

v. to do a physical activity   (syn) practice
n. a physical activity
exercise regularly → We should **exercise** regularly.
do exercise → She usually does **exercise** at the park.

8

favorite
[féivərit]

adj. being liked the most
n. a person or thing one likes the most
favorite subject → My **favorite** subject at school is science.
personal favorite → This movie is my personal **favorite**.

9

festival
[féstivəl]

n. a series of special events to celebrate a particular thing   (syn) celebration
hold a festival
→ My town holds a **festival** each spring.

10

instrument
[ínstrəmənt]

n. a tool used to do something; a tool that plays music
musical instrument
→ Can you play any musical **instruments**?

11 magazine
[mǽgəziːn]

n. a weekly or monthly publication with stories and pictures   (syn) journal

sports magazine

→ I enjoy reading sports **magazines**.

12 musician
[mju(ː)zíʃən]

n. a person who makes music

famous musician

→ Janet wants to become a famous **musician**.

13 participate
[pɑːrtísipèit]

v. to take part in an activity   (syn) join

participate in

→ Everyone should **participate** in the discussion.

14 photo
[fóutou]

n. a picture

take a photo

→ She likes taking **photos** on her smartphone.

15 pleasure
[pléʒər]
v. please

n. a feeling of happiness

for pleasure

→ Many people read books for **pleasure**.

16 puzzle
[pʌ́zl]

n. a toy or problem that is hard to solve; something hard to understand or solve
(syn) riddle

crossword puzzle

→ I like to do crossword **puzzles**.

17 recipe
[résəpì]

n. instructions on how to cook food

follow a recipe

→ Follow the **recipe** to make spaghetti.

18 travel
[trǽvəl]
n. traveler

v. to go from one place to another; to take a trip
n. the act of taking a trip

travel around the world → I hope to **travel** around the world someday.
travel agency → She works for a **travel** agency.

19 volunteer
[vùləntíər]

v. to work for free
n. a person who works for free

volunteer at a library → Steve **volunteers** at the library each Saturday.
hospital volunteer → There are several hospital **volunteers**.

20 walk
[wɔːk]

v. to use one's feet to move slowly
n. the act of using one's feet to move slowly

walk home → I **walk** home from school every day.
take a walk → His family likes to take **walks** in the park.

A **Match the words with their definitions.**

1. act •   • a. to play in a movie, musical, etc.

2. costume •   • b. to work for free

3. instrument •   • c. the act of using one's feet to move slowly

4. cartoon •   • d. special clothes people wear at events

5. bake •   • e. a funny drawing in a newspaper

6. volunteer •   • f. to cook in an oven

7. walk •   • g. a tool used to do something

8. puzzle •   • h. something hard to understand or solve

B **Circle the two words in each group that have the same meaning.**

1. a. exercise b. bake c. practice d. act

2. a. instrument b. festival c. pleasure d. celebration

3. a. collect b. travel c. join d. participate

4. a. magazine b. photo c. puzzle d. journal

C **Circle the words that best fit the sentences.**

1. Many people will participate | bake in the festival.

2. Let's collect | travel to France this summer vacation.

3. The musician | magazine can play three musical instruments.

4. All the zoo animals are in cages | costumes .

5. They take recipe | pleasure in playing computer games.

6. David acts | exercises in the new science-fiction movie.

D Choose the correct words to complete the sentences.

1. Chris likes to _____ stamps and coins.

   a. act   b. walk   c. travel   d. collect

2. My _____ holiday is Thanksgiving.

   a. festival   b. puzzle   c. favorite   d. musician

3. You should _____ regularly for your health.

   a. exercise   b. collect   c. act   d. bake

4. Do you know the _____ for fried chicken?

   a. pleasure   b. recipe   c. cage   d. instrument

5. He can solve a crossword _____ in five minutes.

   a. travel   b. costume   c. photo   d. puzzle

E Read the passage. Then, fill in the blanks.

   Every year, the city of Springfield has a summer **festival**. It is the biggest event of the year. So the city asks for **volunteers** to help. Some people **bake** cakes and cookies. They sell these items at the **festival**. Some people provide **recipes** for special foods. They make these dishes and sell them, too. Other people draw **cartoons** to sell to visitors. Many people in the city **participate** in the **festival**. They help make it a success.

During the **festival**, there are many events. Some people wear special costumes and dance. **Musicians** play various **instruments**. There are also fun contests. Visitors **travel** from far away to see the **festival**. They **walk** around and take **photos**. The **festival** brings **pleasure** to lots of people.

1. The city of Springfield needs _____ for the festival.

2. Some people draw _____ to sell at the festival.

3. Some musicians play _____ for visitors.

4. A lot of people take _____ in the summer festival.

1 alarm
[əlá:rm]

n. a device that sounds when there is danger
fire alarm
→ Buildings must have fire **alarms** in case of fire.

2 asleep
[əslí:p]

adj. sleeping; not awake   (ant) awake
fall asleep
→ I fell **asleep** at 10 last night.

3 awake
[əwéik]

adj. not asleep   (ant) asleep
stay awake
→ I stayed **awake** all night yesterday.

4 breathe
[bri:ð]
n. breath

v. to take air in and out of the body
breathe deeply
→ Sit down and **breathe** deeply.

5 clothes
[klouðz]

n. items people wear on their bodies
put on clothes
→ Put on some **clothes** when you go out.

6 diet
[dáiət]

n. the food a person eats each day
v. to eat less food to lose weight
go on a diet → I decided to go on a **diet**.
diet for one's health → Dad is **dieting** for his health.

7 dish
[diʃ]

n. a container that holds food; food served on a plate   (syn) plate
do the dishes → I will do the **dishes** after dinner.
meat dish → The restaurant specializes in meat **dishes**.

8 feed
[fi:d]
feed - fed - fed

v. to give food to a person or animal; to eat food
feed one's pet → I always **feed** my pet in the morning.
feed on → Whales usually **feed** on squid, octopus, and fish.

9 greet
[gri:t]

v. to say hello to a person
greet one's students
→ Mr. Baker always **greets** his students with a smile.

10 ill
[il]
n. illness

adj. not healthy; not feeling well   (syn) sick   (ant) healthy
fall ill
→ Sam fell **ill** and went to bed early.

11 join
[dʒɔin]

v. to become a member of a group; to connect
join a choir
→ Mary plans to **join** the choir at school.

12 laugh
[læf]
adj. laughing

v. to express happiness by making a loud sound   (ant) cry
n. the act or sound of showing happiness
laugh loudly → We **laughed** loudly at his joke.
give a laugh → Everyone gave a **laugh** at his clothes.

13 moment
[móumənt]

n. a short period of time
in a moment
→ I'll be there in a **moment**.

14 noisy
[nɔ́izi]
n. noise

adj. making a lot of noise   (syn) loud   (ant) quiet
noisy baby
→ John is such a **noisy** baby.

15 question
[kwéstʃən]

n. a sentence that asks for information   (ant) answer
ask a question
→ The teacher wants us to ask **questions**.

16 remember
[rimémbər]

v. to bring something back into one's mind that one already knows   (ant) forget
remember one's name
→ Can you **remember** his name?

17 trash
[træʃ]

n. anything people throw away
trash can
→ Do not put the plastic bottle in the **trash** can.

18 wait
[weit]

v. to do nothing until something happens
wait for
→ We are **waiting** for a bus to come.

19 wear
[weər]
wear - wore - worn

v. to have clothes on one's body   (ant) take off
wear jeans
→ The girl likes to **wear** jeans and a T-shirt.

20 worry
[wʌ́ri]
adj. worried

v. to think about problems a person has
worry about
→ Students often **worry** about their grades.

A Circle the correct definitions for the given words.

1. wait

a. to think about problems a person has   b. to connect

c. to do nothing until something happens   d. to take air in and out of the body

2. awake

a. sleeping   b. not asleep

c. making a lot of noise   d. not healthy

3. dish

a. a container that holds food   b. anything people throw away

c. the food a person eats each day   d. a short period of time

4. ill

a. making a lot of noise   b. not awake

c. a sentence that asks for information   d. not feeling well

B Circle the two words in each group that are opposites.

1. a. remember   b. wait   c. worry   d. forget

2. a. laugh   b. cry   c. join   d. greet

3. a. trash   b. question   c. answer   d. alarm

4. a. ill   b. noisy   c. asleep   d. healthy

C Circle the words that best fit the sentences.

1. Please take out the moment | trash right now.

2. I set my alarm | question for 7:00 AM.

3. You should go on a dish | diet to lose weight.

4. I cannot hear you due to the ill | noisy traffic.

5. Do not feed | greet the animals in the zoo.

6. He fell asleep | awake when the movie started.

D **Choose the correct words to complete the sentences.**

1. Try to _____ slowly when you exercise.
   a. greet   b. breathe   c. feed   d. wait

2. His parents _____ about his grades at school.
   a. worry   b. join   c. diet   d. wear

3. She will buy some _____ to wear to school.
   a. trashes   b. alarms   c. clothes   d. dishes

4. Could you wait a _____, please?
   a. dish   b. moment   c. question   d. diet

5. David will _____ the math club this year.
   a. remember   b. feed   c. laugh   d. join

E **Read the passage. Then, write T for true or F for false.**

Every day, Lisa does the same thing. She wakes up at 7:30 when her **alarm** goes off. She gets up out of bed. She **breathes** deeply for a few **moments**. Next, she puts on her **clothes** and goes to the kitchen. She takes out the **trash**. Then, she puts some dogfood in a **dish** to **feed** her dog. After that, she **greets** her parents by saying, "Good morning," and **joins** her parents for breakfast.

During breakfast, Lisa's mother sometimes asks **questions**. "Do you feel ill? Did you **remember** your homework?" Lisa knows her mother is worried. So she answers all of the **questions**. After breakfast, Lisa gets her backpack. Then, she goes to the bus stop to **wait** for the bus.

1. Lisa needs an alarm to wake up. _____

2. Lisa feeds her cat breakfast every morning. _____

3. Lisa's mother asks her questions at breakfast. _____

4. Lisa takes the subway to school. _____

1	**bark**
	[ba:rk]
		v. to make a sound like a dog
		   bark loudly
		   → The neighbor's dog **barks** loudly at night.

2	**beautiful**
	[bjúːtifl]
	n. beauty
		adj. very pretty (ant) ugly
		   beautiful day
		   → What a **beautiful** day it is!

3	**change**
	[tʃeindʒ]
		v. to become different
		n. the result of something becoming different (syn) difference
		   change into → Caterpillars **change** into butterflies.
		   make a change → We made a **change** in the schedule.

4	**clean**
	[kli:n]
		adj. having no dirt (syn) neat (ant) dirty
		v. to remove the dirt from a place
		   clean and tidy → Keep your room **clean** and tidy.
		   clean one's home → We **clean** our home every weekend.

5	**dangerous**
	[déindʒərəs]
	n. danger
		adj. full of risk (ant) safe
		   dangerous sport
		   → Some people enjoy **dangerous** sports like skiing.

6	**desert**
	[dézərt]
		n. an area of land that gets little or no rain
		   sandy desert
		   → The Sahara is a sandy **desert** in North Africa.

7	**environment**
	[inváirənmənt]
		n. the air, water, land, and everything else in an area
		   protect the environment
		   → We should protect the **environment** for the future.

8	**field**
	[fi:ld]
		n. an area of land used for keeping animals or farming
		   wheat field
		   → The farmer is working in his wheat **field**.

9	**forest**
	[fɔ́(ː)rist]
		n. land with many trees in it (syn) woods
		   forest fire
		   → A **forest** fire burned many trees in the area.

10	**improve**
	[imprúːv]
		v. to make better
		   improve one's health
		   → You can **improve** your health by exercising.

11 lake
[leik]

n. a large body of water with land all around it
in the lake
→ It is dangerous to swim in the **lake**.

12 nest
[nest]

n. a bird's home that it lays its eggs in
build a nest
→ Some birds build **nests** in trees.

13 plant
[plænt]

n. a tree, flower, bush, or grass that grows in the ground
v. to put a tree, flower, bush, or grass into the ground
indoor plants → People keep indoor **plants** to clean the air.
plant a tree → We **planted** a tree on Arbor Day.

14 pollution
[pəlúːʃən]
v. pollute

n. anything that makes the air, water, or soil dirty
air pollution
→ Air **pollution** is a serious problem these days.

15 protect
[prətékt]

v. to keep safe from harm, injury, or damage   *syn* guard   *ant* harm
protect the weak
→ The strong have to **protect** the weak.

16 season
[síːzən]

n. one of the four times of the year when the weather changes
out of season
→ Watermelons are out of **season** in winter.

17 toward
[tɔːrd]

prep. in the direction of
toward one's home
→ We are going **toward** my home now.

18 wild
[waild]

adj. living or growing in natural conditions
wild animal
→ **Wild** animals sometimes appear in this area.

19 wooden
[wúdən]

adj. made of wood
wooden chair
→ My grandpa is sitting in a **wooden** chair.

20 world
[wɜːrld]

n. the Earth
around the world
→ He traveled around the **world** in 80 days.

21

A Circle the words that fit the definitions.

1. to become different

    a. plant   b. change   c. protect   d. bark

2. living or growing in natural conditions

    a. clean   b. dangerous   c. wooden   d. wild

3. a large body of water with land all around it

    a. forest   b. lake   c. world   d. desert

4. made of wood

    a. wooden   b. clean   c. wild   d. beautiful

5. an area of land that gets little or no rain

    a. field   b. season   c. desert   d. nest

B Choose and write the correct words for the blanks.

> forest   clean   beautiful   dangerous   protect   change

1. ugly   ≠ _____

2. safe   ≠ _____

3. dirty   ≠ _____

4. guard   = _____

5. difference   = _____

6. woods   = _____

C Circle the words that best fit the sentences.

1. In December, the season | pollution changes from fall to winter.

2. A changing | barking dog usually does not bite.

3. Billions of people live in the world | change .

4. You need to improve | protect your English.

5. I found a bird's plant | nest in an apple tree.

6. This country has many pine deserts | forests .

D **Choose the correct words to complete the sentences.**

1. Go _____ the lake to get to the supermarket.
   a. clean   b. toward   c. wild   d. wooden

2. All _____ need light and water to grow.
   a. seasons   b. nests   c. lakes   d. plants

3. Some _____ animals are very dangerous.
   a. world   b. toward   c. wooden   d. wild

4. Let's _____ our plans because it is raining.
   a. change   b. protect   c. plant   d. bark

5. We should protect the environment from _____.
   a. field   b. desert   c. pollution   d. nest

E **Read the passage. Then, fill in the blanks.**

 The **world** is full of beauty. There are all kinds of wonderful places. These include **deserts**, mountains, and **forests**. There are also **beautiful lakes**, rivers, and **fields**. But there is a big problem nowadays. People are not **protecting** the **environment**. Instead, they are polluting it. As a result, the world is getting dirty. There are not **clean** rivers, **fields**, and **forests** anymore. It is **dangerous** for our lives.

We need to **change**. We have to save the **environment**. We should reduce the amount of trash. We should also use less plastic. We can **plant** trees and **protect** rainforests to get **clean** air. We need to take care of **wild plants** and animals, too. Then, the **environment** will **improve**. And the **world** will be a more **beautiful** place.

1. The _____ has many wonderful places.

2. _____ is a big problem nowadays.

3. We should change to protect the _____.

4. We should take care of _____ plants and animals.

23

1 activity
[æktívəti]

n. something a person does
outdoor activity
→ Camping is the most popular outdoor **activity.**

2 actually
[ǽktʃuəli]
adj. actual

adv. in fact   (syn) really
actually know
→ Do you **actually** know that famous singer?

3 balance
[bǽləns]

v. to make something steady
n. the act of being steady
balance on one leg → How long can you **balance** on one leg?
lose one's balance → I lost my **balance** and fell off the board.

4 careful
[kéərfl]
adv. carefully

adj. paying attention not to cause harm or damage   (ant) careless
careful driver
→ My mother is a **careful** driver.

5 courage
[kʌ́ridʒ]

n. the ability to face a dangerous situation
full of courage
→ His face is full of **courage** and confidence.

6 creative
[kriéitiv]
v. create

adj. able to think of new ideas
creative mind
→ He makes great art thanks to his **creative** mind.

7 especially
[ispéʃəli]

adv. particularly
especially fun
→ The rollercoaster at the amusement park is **especially** fun.

8 friendly
[fréndli]

adj. being kind or helpful
friendly dog
→ It is a **friendly** dog and does not bite.

9 gesture
[dʒéstʃər]

n. a body movement that has a special meaning
v. to make a body movement that has a special meaning
strange gesture → He often makes strange **gestures.**
gesture for → She **gestured** for me to sit down.

10 habit
[hǽbit]

n. an action a person does regularly
bad habit
→ You should get rid of your bad **habits.**

11 **kind**
[kaind]

adj. gentle, friendly, and caring about others (syn) nice
kind man
→ The **kind** man gave me some food and water.

12 **lazy**
[léizi]

adj. not wanting to do work
lazy person
→ A **lazy** person cannot do anything well.

13 **mental**
[méntəl]

adj. relating to the mind (ant) physical
mental problem
→ That person has a **mental** problem.

14 **mysterious**
[mistí(:)əriəs]
n. mystery

adj. relating to something that is not known or hidden (syn) strange
mysterious smile
→ The *Mona Lisa* has a **mysterious** smile.

15 **person**
[pɜːrsən]

n. a human
kind person
→ Mindy is a very kind **person**.

16 **popular**
[pápjələr]

adj. liked by many people
popular brand
→ This is the most **popular** brand on the market.

17 **quiet**
[kwáiət]

adj. making little or no noise (syn) silent (ant) loud
quiet voice
→ My friend talked to me in a **quiet** voice.

18 **rude**
[ruːd]

adj. having bad manners (ant) polite
rude behavior
→ We were upset by her **rude** behavior.

19 **strong**
[strɔ(:)ŋ]
n. strength

adj. having a lot of physical power; having great power (ant) weak
strong wind
→ A **strong** wind blew over the trees on the street.

20 **unique**
[juːníːk]

adj. very special; like nothing else
unique idea
→ Jason has many **unique** ideas to solve problems.

A Circle the correct definitions for the given words.

1. actually
   a. particularly
   b. in fact
   c. being kind or helpful
   d. making little or no noise

2. person
   a. the act of being steady
   b. having a lot of physical power
   c. a human
   d. something a person does

3. courage
   a. not wanting to do work
   b. an action a person does regularly
   c. making little or no noise
   d. the ability to face a dangerous situation

4. unique
   a. liked by many people
   b. like nothing else
   c. having bad manners
   d. having great power

B Write S for synonym or A for antonym next to each pair of words.

1. _____ rude – polite
2. _____ mysterious – strange
3. _____ quiet – silent
4. _____ mental – physical
5. _____ actually – really
6. _____ strong – weak

C Circle the words that best fit the sentences.

1. We do lots of fun activities | habits at school.

2. I could not understand her balance | gesture at the moment.

3. Stop being lazy | mental and do your homework.

4. Stonehenge is very careful | popular with tourists.

5. Creative | Rude thinking is needed to solve the problem.

6. It is friendly | especially cold in January in this country.

D **Choose the correct words to complete the sentences.**

1. Be _____ not to make mistakes.

a. careful   b. mental   c. mysterious   d. kind

2. His _____ behavior made us angry.

a. creative   b. rude   c. popular   d. actually

3. Look! That person has a _____ hairstyle.

a. lazy   b. friendly   c. quiet   d. unique

4. All people want to break their bad _____.

a. habits   b. courage   c. gestures   d. activities

5. The ballerina has a good sense of _____.

a. gesture   b. mental   c. balance   d. person

E **Read the passage. Then, write T for true or F for false.**

Jason and Steve are good friends. But they are quite different. For example, Jason is a bit **lazy**. He prefers staying home and watching TV. But Steve is very active. He loves to play sports and do outdoor **activities**. Jason is a very **careful person**. He always checks his homework for mistakes. So he gets good grades. Steve is a bit careless though. So his homework is not always good.

Jason is a **quiet** person, but he is **friendly** and **creative**. So he is **popular** with students at school. Steve is **strong** and also has a lot of **courage**. He always helps his weak friends. Many students like him as well. Jason and Steve are different, but they are **especially** good friends. Their friendship is very **mysterious** to their friends.

1. Jason and Steve are good classmates. _____

2. Steve is active and loves to be outdoors. _____

3. Jason is strong and courageous. _____

4. Jason and Steve are popular with students. _____

A   Choose and write the correct words for the definitions.

| pleasure | protect | culture | creative |
| arrive | feed | dangerous | recipe |

1. to get to a place   ➡ _____

2. full of risk   ➡ _____

3. a feeling of happiness   ➡ _____

4. instructions on how to cook food   ➡ _____

5. to give food to a person or animal   ➡ _____

6. to keep safe from harm, injury, or damage   ➡ _____

7. able to think of new ideas   ➡ _____

8. the actions and beliefs of a group of people   ➡ _____

B   Circle the words that are the most similar to the underlined words.

1. Please put some of this food on the <u>plate</u>.
    a. dish   b. backpack   c. magazine   d. instrument

2. The object flying in the sky looks very <u>strange</u>.
    a. creative   b. mysterious   c. unique   d. popular

3. We hope to <u>reach</u> at the train station soon.
    a. travel   b. volunteer   c. arrive   d. participate

4. It is so <u>loud</u> in here because of the TV.
    a. careful   b. mental   c. friendly   d. noisy

5. I often read that <u>comic</u> in the newspaper.
    a. cartoon   b. gesture   c. puzzle   d. festival

C **Choose the correct forms of the words to complete the sentences.**

1. It was my please | pleasure to help you.

2. David became ill | illness three days ago.

3. You should not pollution | pollute the environment.

4. Please do not worried | worry too much about me.

5. They walked careful | carefully through the jungle.

D **Complete the sentences with the words in the box.**

1. Let's _____ some vegetables in the yard.

2. Susan will _____ to help sick people.

3. Tim is _____ good at math and science.

4. The _____ chair is comfortable to sit in.

5. The host _____ everyone at the party with smile.

especially

plant

greets

volunteer

wooden

E **Write the correct phrases in the blanks.**

| foreign country | rude behavior | out of season |
| cartoon characters | art museum | hold a festival |

1. Bella wants to take a trip to a _____ in Asia.

2. Cherries are _____ in winter.

3. Nobody likes his _____ at school.

4. There are many beautiful paintings at the _____ .

5. The town will _____ for five days.

6. Her hobby is drawing _____ .

F **Circle the mistakes. Then, write the correct sentences.**

1. Take a deep breathe and relax.

➡️ _____

2. The desert can be very danger for travelers.

➡️ _____

3. Actual, we are taking a test after lunch.

➡️ _____

4. She bought a cake at the bake.

➡️ _____

5. We had a fantasy time on our trip.

➡️ _____

G **Complete the crossword puzzle.**

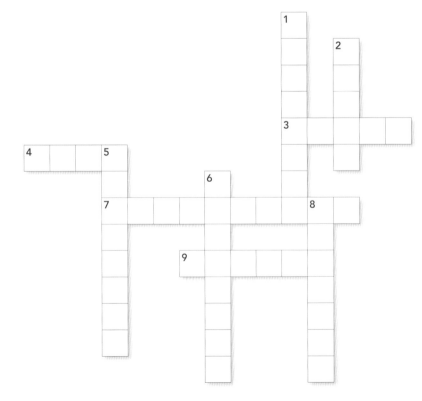

Across

3. anything people throw away

4. to cook in an oven

7. knowledge gained by doing something

9. relating to the mind

Down

1. a sentence that asks for information

2. having no dirt

5. to do a physical activity

6. being kind or helpful

8. the actions and beliefs of a group of people

H Read the passage. Then, answer the questions below.

Visit the Richmond Museum

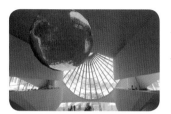

Everyone is welcome to visit the Richmond **Museum**. The **museum** is opening this Saturday, July 10. There are many **fantastic** exhibits to see at the **museum**.

There is an exhibit about the **environment**. Visitors can learn about **deserts**, **lakes**, **forests**, and other places on the Earth. The exhibit shows how **dangerous pollution** is and how harmful it is.

There is an exhibit about Europe, too. Visitors can see **photos** of **palaces** from **foreign countries** and learn about their **cultures**. Visitors can see the music exhibit, too. It has **popular instruments** and music by famous **musicians**.

The **museum** also offers special **activities**. Visitors can go on **adventures** in local areas. They can **walk** through **fields** and **feed** some local animals. It will be a trip to **remember**.

Call 574-3937 for more information.

1. What is the passage mainly about?
   a. a field trip to a museum
   b. a class about the environment
   c. the exhibits at a museum
   d. special activities for students

2. Where can visitors learn about pollution?
   a. at the Europe exhibit
   b. at the environment exhibit
   c. at the music exhibit
   d. at a special activity

3. Which is NOT true about the museum?
   a. It will open soon.
   b. It has various exhibits.
   c. It provides outdoor activities for visitors.
   d. It offers information on its website.

4. What can visitors see at the Europe exhibit?

   ➡️ _____

5. What can visitors do on adventures in local areas?

   ➡️ _____

31

1 adult
[ədʌ́lt]

n. a person who is fully grown   (ant) child
become an adult
→ You will become an **adult** someday.

2 advise
[ədváiz]
n. advice

v. to give an opinion in a particular situation
advise someone
→ My teacher **advised** me on what to do.

3 borrow
[bárou]

v. to use another person's item for a while   (ant) lend
borrow a book
→ Jake **borrowed** a book from the library.

4 build
[bild]
build - built - built

v. to make something   (syn) create
build a bridge
→ They **built** a new bridge over the river.

5 corner
[kɔ́ːrnər]

n. the place where two sides meet
at the corner
→ Turn left at the **corner** and then go straight.

6 decide
[disáid]
n. decision

v. to choose   (syn) determine
decide to go
→ We **decided** to go to the movie theater.

7 effort
[éfərt]

n. the physical or mental energy needed to do something
make an effort
→ She made an **effort** to become a lawyer.

8 exchange
[ikstʃéindʒ]

v. to give something in return for another thing
exchange money
→ I will **exchange** money at the airport.

9 finish
[fíniʃ]

v. to complete something   (syn) end   (ant) begin
finish work
→ My father **finishes** work at six every day.

10 forward
[fɔ́ːrwərd]

adv. toward the front; ahead in time   (ant) backward
look forward to
→ They look **forward** to summer vacation.

11 invite
[inváit]

v. to ask a person to attend an event

invite someone
→ I'd like to **invite** you to a party.

12 letter
[létər]

n. a message written on paper; a symbol used for writing

mail a letter → I'm going to the post office to mail a **letter**.
capital letter → Write your name in capital **letters**.

13 mistake
[mistéik]

n. an incorrect action or opinion

make a mistake
→ Anyone can make a **mistake**.

14 need
[niːd]

v. to want something because it is necessary

need help
→ The poor man **needs** some help.

15 office
[ɔ́(ː)fis]

n. a room in which a person works

office job
→ She wants to get an **office** job at the company.

16 price
[prais]

n. the amount of money something costs

price of oil
→ The **price** of oil has started rising again.

17 report
[ripɔ́ːrt]
n. reporter

v. to give information about something
n. a written account of an event or information

report the news → He **reports** the news on television.
write a report → I wrote a **report** on dinosaurs.

18 traffic
[trǽfik]

n. all the vehicles on the roads

heavy traffic
→ There is heavy **traffic** downtown in the morning.

19 week
[wiːk]
adj. weekly

n. a period of seven days

busy week
→ He has a busy **week** due to his business trip.

20 work
[wəːrk]
n. worker

v. to do one's job
n. an activity that requires physical or mental effort   ⓢⓨⓝ task

work for → My mother **works** for a tour company.
hard work → Preparing for an event is hard **work**.

33

A **Match the words with their definitions.**

1. traffic •   • a. to ask a person to attend an event

2. decide •   • b. a period of seven days

3. invite •   • c. to give an opinion in a particular situation

4. finish •   • d. to complete something

5. adult •   • e. all the vehicles on the roads

6. week •   • f. to want something because it is necessary

7. need •   • g. a person who is fully grown

8. advise •   • h. to choose

B **Circle the two words in each group that have the same meaning.**

1. a. work   b. adult   c. effort   d. task

2. a. borrow   b. build   c. create   d. exchange

3. a. need   b. finish   c. invite   d. end

4. a. determine   b. advise   c. decide   d. report

C **Circle the words that best fit the sentences.**

1. What is the price | work of that computer?

2. Learning a language requires a lot of traffic | effort .

3. The company plans to move to a new office | report downtown.

4. Go forward | mistake to the corner and then turn right.

5. Janet finished | invited Ted to her birthday party.

6. Can I advise | borrow your notebook?

D Choose the correct words to complete the sentences.

1. Mr. Murphy's house is located on the _____.
   a. effort   b. corner   c. mistake   d. report

2. Please write a thank-you _____ to your grandmother.
   a. office   b. price   c. week   d. letter

3. She got an A on her science _____.
   a. report   b. traffic   c. adult   d. price

4. Can I _____ some Korean won for U.S. dollars?
   a. finish   b. build   c. exchange   d. need

5. I won't make the same _____ again.
   a. week   b. mistake   c. adult   d. effort

E Read the passage. Then, fill in the blanks.

My father **works** in an **office** downtown. He goes there every day of the **week**. His company **builds** bridges and buildings. My father **decides** which projects his company will do. Then, he figures out the **price** of each project and writes a **report**.

One time, my father **decided** to **build** a big bridge. But his company did not have enough money. It **needed** money, so my father **advised** the company to **borrow** some money from a bank. There was a big **mistake** when they **built** the bridge. But my father made a big **effort** to fix the **mistake**. Finally, the project **finished** successfully. My father's boss thanked my father. So he wrote him a nice **letter**. He also **invited** my father to meet the company owner.

1. My father's _____ is located downtown.

2. My father's company borrowed money to _____ a bridge.

3. My father fixed a big _____ at his company.

4. My father's boss _____ him to meet the company owner.

Unit 07 Word List

1	**ahead** [əhéd]	*adv.* to the front; in front of straight ahead → Walk straight **ahead** to get to the bank.

2 answer [ǽnsər]
v. to respond to a question (ant) ask
n. a response
answer one's question → Who can **answer** my question?
give an answer → She gave an **answer** to the teacher.

3 award [əwɔ́ːrd]
n. a prize
receive an award
→ He received an **award** for his honesty.

4 class [klæs]
n. classmate
n. a group of students at a school; a time when a teacher teaches students
same class
→ Jacob was in the same **class** last year.

5 college [kálidʒ]
n. a school to study at after high school (syn) university
go to college
→ He studies hard to go to **college**.

6 difficult [dífikəlt]
n. difficulty
adj. not easy to do (syn) hard (ant) simple
difficult problem
→ I cannot solve the **difficult** problem.

7 elementary [èliméntəri]
adj. relating to something simple and basic
elementary school
→ She is a sixth grader in **elementary** school.

8 explain [ikspléin]
v. to talk about something in detail (syn) describe
explain a rule
→ Can you **explain** the rules of chess?

9 fiction [fíkʃən]
n. a story about people or events that are not real
science fiction
→ She loves to read science **fiction**.

10 get [get]
v. to receive; to have something; to become (syn) gain
get a chance → You can **get** a chance to win a prize.
get angry → She **got** angry because of me.

11 **holiday**
[hálədèi]

n. a day honoring a person or event; a day off from work
summer holiday
→ We will take a summer **holiday** next week.

12 **know**
[nou]
know - knew - known

v. to be aware; to understand   (syn) see
know one's address
→ Do you **know** his address?

13 **mind**
[maind]

n. the part of a person that thinks
v. to feel unhappy about something
creative mind → That writer has a creative **mind**.
don't mind → I don't **mind** the noise.

14 **opinion**
[əpínjən]

n. feelings or thoughts about something   (syn) view
give an opinion
→ Please give your **opinion** on this matter.

15 **play**
[plei]
n. player

v. to do things for pleasure; to do a sport or game
n. a performance on stage
play with → She likes to **play** with dolls.
act in a play → She will act in a **play** this summer.

16 **problem**
[prábləm]

n. something that causes trouble   (syn) difficulty
serious problem
→ It may cause a serious **problem**.

17 **share**
[ʃeər]

v. to use something with another person
share a toy
→ Children do not like to **share** their toys.

18 **student**
[stʃúːdənt]
v. study

n. a person who studies at a school
good student
→ A good **student** gets an A⁺ on her test.

19 **vote**
[vout]

v. to take part in an election
vote for president
→ All citizens should **vote** for president.

20 **year**
[jiər]

n. a period lasting 365 days
all year round
→ This country is warm and humid all **year** round.

Unit 07

37

Unit 07 Exercise

A **Circle the words that fit the definitions.**

1. a story about people or events that are not real

    a. answer   b. fiction   c. class   d. problem

2. to use something with another person

    a. vote   b. get   c. share   d. explain

3. to do things for pleasure

    a. play   b. know   c. answer   d. vote

4. relating to something simple and basic

    a. ahead   b. difficult   c. mind   d. elementary

5. a person who studies at a school

    a. college   b. student   c. holiday   d. year

B **Choose and write the correct words for the blanks.**

| explain | problem | know | difficult | college | answer |

1. ask   ≠ _____

2. simple   ≠ _____

3. see   = _____

4. describe   = _____

5. difficulty   = _____

6. university   = _____

C **Circle the words that best fit the sentences.**

1. Paul won an award | answer in the science fair.

2. They will be in the fifth grade all holiday | year long.

3. In my opinion | fiction , this is the correct answer.

4. You need to go straight difficult | ahead to the corner.

5. Children need to learn to mind | share with others.

6. David hopes to get | know a bike for his birthday.

D **Choose the correct words to complete the sentences.**

1. There are more than thirty students in the _____.

   a. answer   b. class   c. mind   d. year

2. Someone should _____ how to use the computer.

   a. get   b. vote   c. mind   d. explain

3. Where did you go on your last _____?

   a. holiday   b. award   c. opinion   d. student

4. Sophia is taking an _____ course on computers.

   a. ahead   b. problem   c. elementary   d. fiction

5. The people _____ for president every four years.

   a. vote   b. know   c. play   d. share

E **Read the passage. Then, write T for true or F for false.**

The **students** at Central **Elementary** School are excited. It is a very important day at the school. They are having school elections today. The **students** must **vote** for the school president.

There are three **students** running for president. They make speeches in front of the other **students**. They **explain** what they will do for the school and the **students**. One **student** wants to improve school lunches. Another wants to **play** more sports after **class**. A third **student** wants to solve **problems** like dirty classrooms.

The other **students** listen carefully and **share** their **opinions**. Then, it is time to decide. Some of them change their **minds** at the end. Now all the **students** are ready to **vote**. They hope a good person becomes the school president this **year**.

1. The school elections at Central Elementary School are tomorrow. _____

2. Three students want to be the school president. _____

3. One student thinks dirty classrooms are a problem. _____

4. No students change their minds before they vote. _____

1	**afraid** [əfréid]	*adj.* showing or feeling fear (ant) brave afraid of → The boy is **afraid** of dogs.
2	**blind** [blaind]	*adj.* unable to see blind man → The **blind** man needed help crossing the street.
3	**comfortable** [kʌ́mfərtəbl] *n.* comfort	*adj.* feeling good or pleasant comfortable shoes → You need **comfortable** shoes for jogging.
4	**enjoy** [indʒɔ́i]	*v.* to have fun doing an activity (syn) like (ant) hate enjoy sports → The boys **enjoy** sports like baseball.
5	**enough** [inʌ́f]	*adj.* having a needed amount of something (syn) plenty enough money → Do you have **enough** money for your trip?
6	**feel** [fi:l] *n.* feeling feel - felt - felt	*v.* to touch with a body part; to have a certain feeling feel smooth → The silk scarf **feels** really smooth. feel happy → The people **felt** happy at the news.
7	**harmony** [háːrməni]	*n.* a state of being peaceful and in agreement in harmony → The choir members are singing in **harmony**.
8	**hungry** [hʌ́ŋgri] *n.* hunger	*adj.* feeling like one needs to eat (ant) full feel hungry → I ate very much, but I still feel **hungry**.
9	**maybe** [méibiː]	*adv.* perhaps (syn) possibly maybe I will → **Maybe** I will go to the library tomorrow.
10	**muscle** [mʌ́sl]	*n.* a body part for controlling movement pull a muscle → I pulled a **muscle** while playing basketball.

Unit 08

11 nervous
[nɜ́ːrvəs]

adj. very worried about something   (syn) anxious
nervous about
→ Lisa is **nervous** about giving a speech.

12 plate
[pleit]

n. a round, flat dish
clean one's plate
→ Please clean your **plate** after you eat.

13 poem
[póuəm]
n. poet

n. a piece of writing, often with rhyming words
write a poem
→ He wrote a **poem** for his parents.

14 pure
[pjuər]

adj. not mixed with anything else   (syn) clean
pure gold
→ The necklace is made of 100% **pure** gold.

15 reduce
[ridʒúːs]

v. to lower in number or amount
reduce a cost
→ The company wants to **reduce** costs.

16 shake
[ʃeik]
shake - shook - shaken

v. to move back and forth, often quickly   (syn) wave
shake hands
→ People **shake** hands when they meet.

17 skin
[skin]

n. the outer part of the body
soft skin
→ The woman has beautiful soft **skin**.

18 sweet
[swiːt]

adj. having a taste like sugar
sweet food
→ Do not eat too much **sweet** food.

19 touch
[tʌtʃ]

v. to put one's hand or finger on someone or something
touch one's face
→ He is always **touching** his face.

20 view
[vjuː]
n. viewer

n. what one can see from a place; a personal belief   (syn) opinion
great view → There is a great **view** from the mountain.
point of view → They have different points of **view**.

A Circle the words that fit the definitions.

1. to touch with a body part

a. reduce   b. feel   c. shake   d. enjoy

2. a state of being peaceful and in agreement

a. harmony   b. view   c. plate   d. skin

3. to lower in number or amount

a. shake   b. enjoy   c. touch   d. reduce

4. not mixed with anything else

a. sweet   b. blind   c. pure   d. afraid

5. a piece of writing, often with rhyming words

a. skin   b. poem   c. muscle   d. plate

B Write S for synonym or A for antonym next to each pair of words.

1. _____ nervous – anxious   **2.** _____ enjoy – hate

3. _____ afraid – brave   **4.** _____ hungry – full

5. _____ maybe – possibly   **6.** _____ view – opinion

C Circle the words that best fit the sentences.

1. My mom doesn't like sweet | nervous things like chocolate.

2. Reduce | Shake the bottle before you take a drink.

3. All of the rooms at the hotel have an ocean view | poem .

4. The weightlifter has big muscles | skin .

5. We don't have afraid | enough time to finish the work.

6. This shirt is made of 100% hungry | pure cotton.

D Choose the correct words to complete the sentences.

1. Don't _____ the pictures at the museum.

   a. enjoy   b. reduce   c. touch   d. shake

2. You have a red spot on your _____.

   a. harmony   b. skin   c. muscle   d. poem

3. This sofa is so _____ to sit on

   a. nervous   b. pure   c. hungry   d. comfortable

4. Helen Keller went _____ when she was young.

   a. blind   b. sweet   c. afraid   d. enough

5. There is some delicious food on the _____.

   a. view   b. harmony   c. plate   d. skin

E Read the passage. Then, fill in the blanks.

This morning, Susan is **nervous**. Her mother is preparing her breakfast. There are some bacon and eggs on her **plate**. However, she doesn't **feel hungry** and doesn't want to eat anything. Her mother asks her if she is sick. She **touches** Susan's forehead. Her **skin** is cold and wet. Susan is **shaking**, too.

"What's the matter?" she asks her daughter. "I am **afraid**," she answers. "I have to read a **poem** in class in front of all the students." Susan's mother tells her not to worry and to **enjoy** reading the **poem**. She asks Susan to read the **poem** for her. When Susan finishes, her mother looks happy. She says, "I believe you will do well today." Now Susan **feels** more **comfortable**.

1. Susan doesn't feel _____ at breakfast.

2. Susan's _____ is cold, and her body is shaking.

3. Susan is afraid about reading a _____ in class.

4. Susan feels _____ after reading the poem to her mother.

1 bath
[bæθ]

n. an act of washing oneself in a bathtub
take a bath
→ I always take a **bath** at night.

2 below
[bilóu]

prep. in a lower place (syn) under (ant) above
below sea level
→ Death Valley is **below** sea level.

3 break
[breik]
break - broke - broken

v. to separate into two or more pieces; to stop working after being damaged (ant) fix
n. a short rest period
break into pieces → The glass fell and **broke** into pieces.
take a break → Let's take a **break**.

4 child
[tʃaild]

n. a young boy or girl (ant) adult
raise a child
→ It is not easy to raise a **child**.

5 diary
[dáiəri]

n. a book in which one writes about one's experiences daily
(syn) journal
keep a diary
→ Janet keeps a **diary** in English.

6 fair
[feər]

adj. proper; treating all equally according to the rules
fair decision
→ The judges made a **fair** decision.

7 floor
[flɔːr]

n. the part of a room people walk on; one level in a building
on the floor → The carpet is laid on the **floor**.
first floor → The hospital is on the first **floor**.

8 guest
[gest]

n. a person who is visiting another one (syn) visitor
invite a guest
→ They will invite many **guests** to their wedding.

9 hometown
[hóumtaun]

n. the place where a person is born or grew up in
leave one's hometown
→ She left her **hometown** to go to college.

10 live
[liv][laiv]

v. to have your home in a certain place; to be alive (ant) die
adj. living (ant) dead
live in → My uncle **lives** in a foreign country.
live animal → There are a lot of **live** animals in the forest.

11 midnight
[mídnàit]

n. twelve o'clock at night   (ant) noon
at midnight
→ He woke up at **midnight**.

12 neighbor
[néibər]

n. neighborhood

n. a person who lives near another one
next-door neighbor
→ Our next-door **neighbor** is very quiet.

13 own
[oun]

n. owner

v. to have something
adj. relating or belong to oneself
own a car → Mr. Smith **owns** a nice car.
one's own room → I have my **own** room at home.

14 quite
[kwait]

adv. to a great degree; completely
quite loud
→ The music at the concert is **quite** loud.

15 safe
[seif]

adv. safely

adj. protected from harm or danger   (ant) dangerous
safe and sound
→ Everybody arrived home **safe** and sound.

16 thing
[θiŋ]

n. a nonliving object
interesting thing
→ I found an interesting **thing** in the closet.

17 town
[taun]

n. a small city where people live and work
local town
→ The local **town** is five kilometers away.

18 upstairs
[ʌpstéərz]

adv. on a higher level of a building   (ant) downstairs
go upstairs
→ Let's go **upstairs** to the second floor.

19 visit
[vízit]

n. visitor

v. to go to a place for a short time
visit one's house
→ I will **visit** your house this weekend.

20 without
[wiðáut]

prep. not having, using, or doing something   (ant) with
do without
→ My father can do **without** a car.

Unit 09 Exercise

A **Circle the correct definitions for the given words.**

1. neighbor
- a. a young boy or girl
- b. a person who lives near another one
- c. one level in a building
- d. twelve o'clock at night

2. fair
- a. proper
- b. in a lower place
- c. to a great degree
- d. relating or belong to oneself

3. visit
- a. to be alive
- b. to separate into two or more pieces
- c. to have something
- d. to go to a place for a short time

4. thing
- a. a short rest period
- b. the part of a room people walk on
- c. a nonliving object
- d. a person who is visiting another one

B **Circle the two words in each group that are opposites.**

1. a. fair   b. dangerous   c. safe   d. live

2. a. live   b. floor   c. die   d. hometown

3. a. quite   b. fair   c. above   d. below

4. a. child   b. neighbor   c. guest   d. adult

C **Circle the words that best fit the sentences.**

1. Everybody in the town | child loved the boy.

2. She writes in her floor | diary almost every day.

3. I will put on my pajamas after I take a bath | guest .

4. Do you know who broke | lived the window?

5. I think his story is upstairs | quite interesting.

6. Plants can't live below | without sunlight.

46

D **Choose the correct words to complete the sentences.**

1. We are having two _____ for dinner.

  a. towns   b. diaries   c. baths   d. guests

2. My father's _____ is very far from here.

  a. break   b. hometown   c. midnight   d. thing

3. Mr. White lives on the fifth _____ of the building.

  a. floor   b. neighbor   c. break   d. child

4. I saw the accident with my _____ eyes.

  a. fair   b. live   c. own   d. safe

5. I need to go _____ and take a bath.

  a. below   b. without   c. quiet   d. upstairs

E **Read the passage. Then, write T for true or F for false.**

Mr. Smith's **hometown** is a small **town** near a beach. His parents **live** there. So the Smith family decides to **visit** them this summer vacation. Mr. Smith plans to drive his **own** car there. They leave their **town** early in the morning. They sometimes take **breaks** to get snacks. It takes four hours to arrive. Everyone is tired, so they take **baths** and go to bed early.

Suddenly, around **midnight**, Mr. Smith wakes up. It is noisy outside. "What's that noise?" he asks. His parents' **neighbors** are having a party. There are many **guests** at the party. They are dancing and singing on the **floor**. Mr. Smith asks them to be quiet. The next morning, Mr. Smith wakes up late and can't see the sunrise.

1. Mr. Smith's family lives near a beach.   _____

2. It takes four hours to fly to Mr. Smith's hometown.   _____

3. Some loud noise wakes up Mr. Smith.   _____

4. Mr. Smith can't see the sunrise the next morning.   _____

1	**avoid** [əvɔ́id]	*v.* to keep away from someone or something avoid someone → She is always trying to **avoid** me.
2	**battle** [bǽtl]	*n.* a fight between two armies or groups (syn) war survive a battle → Few soldiers survived the **battle**.
3	**beat** [bi:t] beat - beat - beaten	*v.* to hit hard; to defeat someone in a game (ant) lose beat a team → We **beat** the team by two goals.
4	**blood** [blʌd]	*n.* the red liquid that flows through the body lose blood → He lost a lot of **blood** in the accident.
5	**brave** [breiv]	*adj.* not being afraid (ant) scared brave decision → Mr. Lewis made a very **brave** decision.
6	**challenge** [tʃǽlindʒ]	*v.* to try to do something difficult *n.* an effort at doing something difficult challenge someone → He **challenged** me to a fight. accept a challenge → I decided to accept the **challenge**.
7	**dead** [ded] *v.* die	*adj.* no longer living (ant) alive dead body → The police found a **dead** body in the room.
8	**evil** [í:vəl]	*adj.* very bad; morally wrong (ant) good evil man → The **evil** man tried to steal the money.
9	**forever** [fərévər]	*adv.* for all time (syn) always live forever → Nothing on the Earth can live **forever**.
10	**history** [hístəri]	*n.* events that happened in the past world history → We learn world **history** at middle school.

Unit 10

11 kingdom
[kíŋdəm]

n. the land that a king rules

rule a kingdom

→ He ruled his **kingdom** for twenty years.

12 machine
[məʃíːn]

n. equipment that does a particular job   (syn) tool

invent a machine

→ Thomas Edison invented many **machines**.

13 nation
[néiʃən]
adj. national

n. a country

Asian nation

→ China and India are two Asian **nations**.

14 occur
[əkə́ːr]

v. to take place   (syn) happen

often occur

→ Earthquakes often **occur** in this country.

15 place
[pleis]

n. a certain area

quiet place

→ The library is a quiet **place** to study.

16 prepare
[pripéər]

v. to get ready

prepare a test

→ I'm busy **preparing** my test.

17 rule
[ruːl]

n. directions or a law
v. to have power over people or a group

follow a rule → Please follow the **rules** of the game.
rule a country → The king **ruled** the country wisely.

18 ship
[ʃip]

n. a very large boat used to carry people or goods

sailing ship

→ I traveled to the island on a sailing **ship**.

19 symbol
[símbəl]
v. symbolize

n. a picture or shape with a special meaning   (syn) sign

symbol of peace

→ A dove is a **symbol** of peace.

20 tough
[tʌf]

adj. difficult; strong when dealing with hard situations   (ant) weak

tough time

→ Janet had a **tough** time yesterday.

49

A **Match the words with their definitions.**

1. blood   •

2. rule   •

3. machine   •

4. prepare   •

5. history   •

6. challenge   •

7. ship   •

8. avoid   •

• a. to get ready

• b. to try to do something difficult

• c. a very large boat used to carry people or goods

• d. directions or a law

• e. events that happened in the past

• f. the red liquid that flows through the body

• g. to keep away from someone or something

• h. equipment that does a particular job

B **Write S for synonym or A for antonym next to each pair or words.**

1. _____ tough – weak

2. _____ evil – good

3. _____ battle – war

4. _____ machine – tool

5. _____ dead – alive

6. _____ occur – happen

C **Circle the words that best fit the sentences.**

1. We should avoid | prepare for Tom's birthday party.

2. He comes from a nation | battle far away.

3. The brave | dead firefighter ran into the burning building.

4. The boy occurred | challenged the bully to a fight.

5. The bull is a place | symbol of strength.

6. She uses a washing machine | ship to do laundry.

D Choose the correct words to complete the sentences.

1. Some people believe the universe will last _____.

    a. tough   b. forever   c. dead   d. evil

2. He rules over a large _____ in Africa.

    a. battle   b. symbol   c. kingdom   d. machine

3. I _____ going shopping on Saturdays.

    a. avoid   b. beat   c. occur   d. rule

4. We should find a _____ to have lunch soon.

    a. place   b. blood   c. machine   d. rule

5. You have to _____ the drum to make music with it.

    a. rule   b. challenge   c. occur   d. beat

E Read the passage. Then, fill in the blanks.

According to stories, King Arthur **ruled** England hundreds of years ago. He was one of the greatest kings in English **history**. His **kingdom** was very powerful. Today, he is a hero in his **nation**.

King Arthur **ruled** his **kingdom** very well. He made sure everyone followed the **rules**. He was a **tough** man. He was a **brave** man, too. He did not **avoid battles**. Instead, he often fought **battles** against his enemies. He told his soldiers to **prepare** for war at any time. His soldiers **challenged evil** people everywhere. They won many **battles** against their enemies.

Sadly, King Arthur did not live **forever**. He died during a **battle**. King Arthur was very important to England. Because of that, people still remember him today.

1. King Arthur was a great king in English _____.

2. King Arthur was a _____ and brave man.

3. King Arthur and his soldiers won _____ against their enemies.

4. King Arthur did not live _____, but people still remember him.

A Choose and write the correct words for the definitions.

beat	hungry	brave	explain
upstairs	afraid	exchange	fair

1. not being afraid ➡ _____

2. to talk about something in detail ➡ _____

3. treating all equally according to the rules ➡ _____

4. showing or feeling fear ➡ _____

5. to give something in return for another thing ➡ _____

6. to defeat someone in a game ➡ _____

7. feeling like one needs to eat ➡ _____

8. on a higher level of a building ➡ _____

B Circle the words that are the most similar to the underlined words.

1. Sue really <u>likes</u> playing games with her friends.
   a. reduces   b. enjoys   c. feels   d. shakes

2. They will fix the equipment by using a <u>tool</u>.
   a. machine   b. symbol   c. battle   d. rule

3. The project is going to <u>end</u> soon.
   a. invite   b. work   c. finish   d. borrow

4. A <u>visitor</u> is coming to our house for dinner.
   a. child   b. guest   c. thing   d. neighbor

5. Tom gave his <u>view</u> on the news report.
   a. fiction   b. award   c. answer   d. opinion

C Choose the correct forms of the words to complete the sentences.

1. John had some difficult | difficulty in his math class.

2. The French nation | national team won the soccer game.

3. The teacher often advises | advices students about their future.

4. I feel comfort | comfortable when I am at home.

5. Kristina likes to visit | visitor her grandparents every weekend.

D Complete the sentences with the words in the box.

1. The _____ of gold is going up nowadays.

2. We should _____ the amount of water we use.

3. A person cannot live _____.

4. They plan to watch a _____ at the theater.

5. All the people on the ship were _____ from the storm.

| forever |
| safe |
| price |
| reduce |
| play |

E Write the correct phrases in the blanks.

| don't mind | follow the rules | office job |
| heavy traffic | take a bath | shake hands |

1. I _____ if you use my computer.

2. You should _____ after you arrive at home.

3. George wants an _____ after he finishes college.

4. He was glad to _____ with the president.

5. Please _____ at the museum.

6. The _____ made Ken late for school.

F **Circle the mistakes. Then, write the correct sentences.**

1. Let's student together after school.

    ➡ _____

2. A heart is a symbolize of love.

    ➡ _____

3. Everyone on the plane was safely.

    ➡ _____

4. Mr. Taylor will decision on the plan tomorrow.

    ➡ _____

5. Every student had to write a poet for English class.

    ➡ _____

G **Complete the crossword puzzle.**

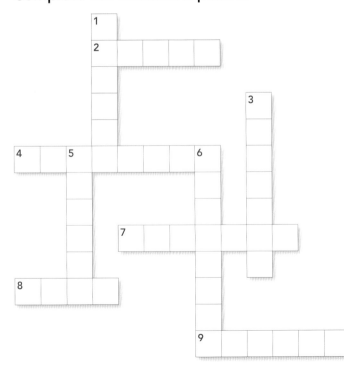

Across

2. to the front; in front of
4. the place where a person is born or grew up in
7. the land that a king rules
8. to want something because it is necessary
9. to lower in number or amount

Down

1. a fight between two armies or groups
3. feelings or thoughts about something
5. a body part for controlling movement
6. a person who lives near another one

H **Read the passage. Then, answer the questions below.**

Life in the Past

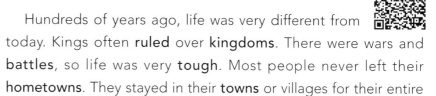

Hundreds of years ago, life was very different from today. Kings often **ruled** over **kingdoms**. There were wars and **battles**, so life was very **tough**. Most people never left their **hometowns**. They stayed in their **towns** or villages for their entire lives.

Their lives were not **comfortable** either. In fact, they were quite **difficult**. People had to **work** every day of the **week**. Most of them were farmers, so they **worked** hard in their fields. Few people went to **college**. Most people just **knew** a few **elementary** facts.

Then, in the 1700s, something interesting **occurred**: people began making **machines**. This began the Industrial Revolution. People started using **machines** to do **work**. They made people's lives easier. People had more times for themselves. They could start to **enjoy** their lives.

1. What is the passage mainly about?

    a. the Industrial Revolution

    b. why people like machines

    c. people's lives in the past

    d. where most people lived

2. What is true about most people in the past?

    a. They had easy lives.   b. They went to college.

    c. They knew a lot of things.   d. They stayed in their hometowns.

3. What did people do in the 1700s?

    a. They made machines.   b. They moved to new villages.

    c. They learned elementary facts.   d. They worked in their offices.

4. Why was life very tough in the past?

    ➡ _____

5. How did machines help people?

    ➡ _____

1	**accept** [əksépt]	*v.* to take something; to agree (syn) receive accept advice → He won't **accept** advice from you.

2	**attend** [əténd] *n.* attention	*v.* to be present at an event attend school → Students must **attend** school on weekdays.

3	**between** [bitwíːn]	*prep.* in the space separating two things or people (syn) among between A and B → It's a secret **between** you and me.

4	**bring** [briŋ] bring - brought - brought	*v.* to take something to a place (syn) carry bring an umbrella → Don't forget to **bring** an umbrella.

5	**call** [kɔːl]	*v.* to telephone someone; to speak in a loud voice (syn) shout call on the phone → Susan **called** her friend on the phone. call one's name → He **called** our names one by one.

6	**communicate** [kəmjúːnikèit] *n.* communication	*v.* to exchange information or thoughts with someone (syn) contact communicate by email → We often **communicate** by email.

7	**deliver** [dilívər] *n.* delivery	*v.* to take an item to another person deliver a letter → The mailman **delivers** letters to people daily.

8	**donate** [dóuneit] *n.* donation	*v.* to give money or something else to help others donate money → He **donates** money to the poor.

9	**favor** [féivər]	*n.* something done out of kindness do a favor → Would you do me a **favor**?

10	**forgive** [fərgív] forgive - forgave - forgiven	*v.* to stop being upset with a person who has hurt one (syn) excuse forgive a friend → She **forgave** her friend for lying to her.

11 **gather**
[gǽðər]

v. to bring together in one place   (syn) collect
  gather together
  → Everyone **gathered** together at the restaurant.

---

12 **leader**
[líːdər]
v. lead

n. a person who leads a group of people
  follow the leader
  → We should follow the **leader** at all times.

---

13 **master**
[mǽstər]

n. a person who is very good at something
v. to learn a skill very well
  taekwondo master → The taekwondo **master** has a black belt.
  master English → It is impossible to **master** English quickly.

---

14 **promise**
[prámis]

v. to say that one will do something
n. a statement that one will do something
  promise to meet → We **promised** to meet at 6:00.
  break a promise → You should never break a **promise**.

---

15 **repeat**
[ripíːt]

v. to do or say again
  repeat after someone
  → The teacher told the students to **repeat** after her.

---

16 **speak**
[spiːk]

n. speech
speak - spoke - spoken

v. to talk to someone about something   (syn) say
  speak slowly
  → Try to **speak** slowly in public.

---

17 **suddenly**
[sʌ́dnli]

adv. without warning
  suddenly happen
  → The accident **suddenly** happened last night.

---

18 **teach**
[tiːtʃ]

n. teacher
teach - taught - taught

v. to give lessons to students at a school
  teach science
  → Mr. Patterson **teaches** science at a school.

---

19 **together**
[təgéðər]

adv. into one group   (ant) alone
  work together
  → They work **together** all day long.

---

20 **welcome**
[wélkəm]

v. to greet a person kindly
  welcome a guest
  → The host **welcomed** the guests with a smile.

A   **Circle the correct definitions for the given words.**

1. donate
   a. to agree
   b. to talk to someone about something
   c. to learn a skill very well
   d. to give money or something else to help others

2. call
   a. to speak in a loud voice
   b. to take an item to another person
   c. to greet a person kindly
   d. to give lessons to students at a school

3. promise
   a. to be present at an event
   b. to do or say again
   c. to say that one will do something
   d. to bring together in one place

4. welcome
   a. to take something
   b. to greet a person kindly
   c. to telephone someone
   d. to talk to someone about something

B   **Circle the two words in each group that have the same meaning.**

1. a. bring   b. communicate   c. teach   d. carry

2. a. gather   b. forgive   c. excuse   d. repeat

3. a. between   b. forever   c. among   d. favor

4. a. gather   b. collect   c. attend   d. master

C   **Circle the words that best fit the sentences.**

1. Please attend | forgive me for forgetting your birthday.

2. Could you please do a favor | leader for me?

3. I together | suddenly remembered to do my homework.

4. Many people deliver | communicate by email these days.

5. Could you please repeat | gather what you said?

6. That man is a promise | master of the piano.

D **Choose the correct words to complete the sentences.**

1. The students are working _____ on their project.

    a. between   b. suddenly   c. gather   d. together

2. How many people will _____ the party?

    a. attend   b. bring   c. communicate   d. forgive

3. The mailman will _____ the package soon.

    a. repeat   b. welcome   c. deliver   d. teach

4. I will _____ your decision about the plan.

    a. call   b. accept   c. gather   d. master

5. Are you able to _____ a foreign language?

    a. speak   b. bring   c. donate   d. welcome

E **Read the passage. Then, write T for true or F for false.**

This evening, a special event will take place at the community center. The city mayor will meet with local residents. He wants to **communicate** with them.

The meeting starts at six o'clock. But the mayor arrives at the community center early. He **welcomes** each person there. More than 200 people **gather** at the community center. They want to hear their **leader speak**.

The mayor begins to **speak**. **Suddenly**, the power goes out. So people cannot hear him. After the power goes back on, the mayor **repeats** his comments. He asks the residents for a **favor**. He wants to improve the community. So he asks the people to **donate** their time and money to the poor. People **accept** his idea and **promise** to help others.

1. The mayor arrives at the community center at six o'clock. _____

2. More than 200 people attend the meeting. _____

3. The power goes out after the mayor's speech. _____

4. The people promise to donate money to the poor. _____

1 access
[ǽksès]

v. to be able to use something
n. the right to use something

access a website → Anyone can **access** the website.
gain access to → Did you gain **access** to the room?

---

2 board
[bɔːrd]

v. to get on a ship, plane, or train
n. a flat surface used to play games on

board a plane → I will **board** the plane in ten minutes.
board game → We enjoy playing **board** games during breaks.

---

3 character
[kǽriktər]

n. the quality of someone or something; a person in a book or play

good character → Mr. White is a man of good **character**.
main character → Who is the main **character** in the movie?

---

4 choose
[tʃuːz]

n. choice
choose - chose - chosen

v. to pick one thing instead of another

choose a number
→ **Choose** a number between one and ten.

---

5 during
[djú(ː)əriŋ]

prep. throughout a period of time

during the break
→ She took a nap **during** the break.

---

6 fight
[fait]

n. fighter
fight - fought - fought

v. to take part in a battle against an enemy
n. a battle

fight a war → The soldiers **fought** the war bravely.
get in a fight → They got in a **fight** after school.

---

7 find
[faind]

find - found - found

v. to search for something successfully   (ant) lose

find money
→ I **found** some money on the street today.

---

8 impossible
[impásəbl]

adj. unable to be done or to happen   (ant) possible

impossible dream
→ It sounds like an **impossible** dream.

---

9 limit
[límit]

n. the greatest amount or degree of something possible

speed limit
→ The speed **limit** on the road is 70 kilometers per hour.

---

10 match
[mætʃ]

n. a game   (syn) contest
v. to find two things that are the same

win a match → The team hopes to win the **match** tonight.
match cards → **Match** the cards when playing this game.

11	**miss** [mis]	*v.* to fail to hit or get something; to want to see someone very much

miss a bus → Paul got up late and **missed** the bus.

miss a friend → I **miss** my friend Kevin very much.

12	**overcome** [òuvərkám] overcome - overcame - overcome	*v.* to succeed in dealing with a problem (syn) beat (ant) lose

overcome a problem

→ Chris **overcame** his problems at school.

13	**pity** [píti]	*v.* to feel sorry for someone *n.* a feeling of sorrow for someone

pity someone → I **pity** the poor in my city.

feel pity for → She felt **pity** for the old woman.

14	**prize** [praiz]	*n.* something a person receives after winning a contest (syn) award

win a prize

→ The best player will win a **prize**.

15	**ready** [rédi]	*adj.* prepared for something that will happen

ready to go

→ Are you **ready** to go to school now?

16	**signal** [sígnəl]	*n.* something that warns or directs others (syn) sign *v.* to warn, give directions, or gesture

traffic signal → The traffic **signal** just turned green.

signal someone → The police officer **signaled** him to stop.

17	**speed** [spi:d]	*n.* how fast someone or something is moving

top speed

→ The man drove his car at top **speed**.

18	**twice** [twais]	*adv.* two times

twice a month

→ My family eats out **twice** a month.

19	**useful** [jú:sfəl] *v.* use	*adj.* helpful at doing something (ant) useless

useful advice

→ My teacher gave me some **useful** advice.

20	**wish** [wiʃ]	*v.* to want something to happen (syn) hope *n.* a feeling that you want something

wish for → She **wishes** for an A⁺ on the test.

make a wish → The genie told Aladdin to make a **wish**.

A   Circle the words that fit the definitions.

1. prepared for something that will happen

     a. useful   b. ready   c. impossible   d. twice

2. to feel sorry for someone

     a. wish   b. signal   c. overcome   d. pity

3. a flat surface used to play games on

     a. limit   b. board   c. fight   d. character

4. to pick one thing instead of another

     a. access   b. match   c. choose   d. find

B   Choose and write the correct words for the blanks.

match	useful	prize	overcome	find	impossible

1. possible ≠ _____   2. useless ≠ _____

3. award = _____   4. lose   ≠ _____

5. beat   = _____   6. contest = _____

C   Circle the words that best fit the sentences.

1. He swung hard but missed | wished the ball.

2. Sarah had a fight | signal with her sister yesterday.

3. He matches | wishes everyone a very happy new year.

4. What is the fastest pity | speed of this car?

5. The wind blew strongly during | twice the storm.

6. Please do not go faster than the speed access | limit .

D **Choose the correct words to complete the sentences.**

1. A green light is a _____ to go.

a. signal   b. prize   c. match   d. board

2. You need a password to get _____ to the computer.

a. character   b. limit   c. access   d. fight

3. You should knock on the door _____.

a. impossible   b. useful   c. ready   d. twice

4. The man _____ his problems and was successful.

a. overcame   b. chose   c. boarded   d. wished

5. What is the name of your favorite cartoon _____?

a. board   b. character   c. speed   d. pity

E **Read the passage. Then, fill in the blanks.**

Chris is a professional gamer. He plays **board** games and computer games. A big computer game **match** is coming, and he is **ready**.

It is the day of the **match**. Chris's friends and family members are there. They **wish** him good luck before the **match** starts. Everyone **chooses** a **character** before the game starts. Then, the referee gives a **signal**. There is a 30-minute time **limit** for the game.

The players start **fighting** monsters. Chris starts off poorly, so he has to **overcome** his low score. It looks **impossible** for him to win. But he starts playing better. He passes the other players. The referee blows the whistle. The game is over. Chris has won the **match**. He wins first **prize**.

1. Chris is _____ to play the big computer game match.

2. Chris's friends and family members _____ him good luck.

3. The players have a 30-minute time _____ to fight monsters.

4. Chris wins the match and gets first _____.

1	**add** [æd] *n.* addition	*v.* to put numbers together to get a total; to put something with another thing add numbers → Anna can **add** numbers very quickly.
2	**calendar** [kǽlindər]	*n.* a chart showing the days, weeks, and months of a year check a calendar → Let me check the **calendar** before fixing the date.
3	**circle** [sɜ́:rkl]	*n.* a completely round shape *v.* to make a completely round shape draw a circle → Draw a **circle** on the paper. circle an answer → Please **circle** the answers on the test.
4	**count** [kaunt]	*v.* to say numbers in order; to add up the number of things count down → They **counted** down from ten to one on New Year's Eve.
5	**degree** [digrí:]	*n.* a unit for measuring something; the level of something high degree → Cook the food at a high **degree** Celsius.
6	**empty** [émpti]	*adj.* having nothing inside syn blank ant full empty bottle → Throw the **empty** bottle in the trash can.
7	**half** [hæf]	*n.* one of two equal parts half an hour → The clock is **half** an hour fast.
8	**height** [hait] *adj.* high	*n.* the degree of how tall a person or thing is in height → The tower is almost 15 meters in **height**.
9	**inside** [insáid]	*prep.* in the inner part of something ant outside *adv.* indoors inside a box → The cat is hiding **inside** a box. go inside → We have to go **inside** because of the rain.
10	**learn** [lɜ́:rn]	*v.* to gain knowledge or skill syn study learn a language → It is not easy to **learn** a foreign language.

11 lesson
[lésən]

n. a period of time when people study
piano lesson
→ Heather takes piano **lessons** twice a week.

12 math
[mæθ]

n. the study of numbers and shapes [syn] mathematics
be good at math
→ Larry is very good at **math**.

13 practice
[prǽktis]

v. to repeat an activity to learn it better [syn] exercise
practice every day
→ It is important to **practice** every day.

14 sign
[sain]

n. a mark, shape, or event that has a meaning [syn] signal
v. to write one's name on something
stop sign → There is a stop **sign** at the corner of the road.
sign one's name → He **signed** his name on the paper.

15 spend
[spend]
spend - spent - spent

v. to use money; to use time doing something [ant] save
spend time on
→ He **spends** too much time watching TV.

16 straight
[streit]

adj. without a bend or curve
adv. not in a curve or at an angle
straight line → Draw a **straight** line between the two points.
walk straight → Walk **straight** for two blocks.

17 temperature
[témpərətʃər]

n. the measure of how hot or cold something is
high temperature
→ The oven is cooking food at a high **temperature**.

18 thousand
[θáuzənd]

n. the number 1,000
thousands of
→ The car costs **thousands** of dollars.

19 weigh
[wei]
n. weight

v. to measure how heavy or light something is
weigh a ton
→ The boxes **weigh** a ton.

20 wrong
[rɔ(:)ŋ]

adj. not right or correct
wrong answer
→ The girl wrote no **wrong** answers on her test.

A **Match the words with their definitions.**

1. weigh • • a. the measure of how hot or cold something is

2. learn • • b. to gain knowledge or skill

3. calendar • • c. a completely round shape

4. circle • • d. to measure how heavy or light something is

5. temperature • • e. the study of numbers and shapes

6. wrong • • f. the degree of how tall a person or thing is

7. math • • g. a chart showing the days, weeks, and months of a year

8. height • • h. not right or correct

B **Write S for synonym or A for antonym next to each pair of words.**

1. _____ learn – study   2. _____ empty – full

3. _____ inside – outside   4. _____ sign – signal

5. _____ practice – exercise 6. _____ spend – save

C **Circle the words that best fit the sentences.**

1. She has a swimming lesson | math after school.

2. The doctor took the boy's sign | temperature to check for a fever.

3. My mom has curly hair, but I have wrong | straight hair.

4. The boy can weigh | count up to ten in Chinese.

5. Cut the pie in half | height and share it with your sister.

6. Cook the meat at 350 degrees | circles for 10 minutes.

D **Choose the correct words to complete the sentences.**

1. You must _____ milk after you mix the flour and sugar.
   a. add   b. weigh   c. circle   d. count

2. All of the rooms in the building are _____.
   a. half   b. wrong   c. empty   d. inside

3. He is driving the _____ way on that street.
   a. height   b. degree   c. wrong   d. lesson

4. How much money did you _____ on that new bike?
   a. learn   b. spend   c. practice   d. sign

5. The little girl can count from one to a _____.
   a. thousand   b. temperature   c. math   d. calendar

E **Read the passage. Then, write T for true or F for false.**

It was the first day of school, and I was worried. My homeroom teacher was Ms. Simmons. She was a **math** teacher. Everyone said she was scary and her **lessons** were hard. All of the students looked nervous. Then, Ms. Simmons came into the classroom.

She introduced herself and started teaching class. We were surprised. We were **wrong**! She was kind, and her **lessons** were wonderful.

For one year, we had a great time in her **math** class. We **learned** how to **count** to one **thousand**. We also **learned** to **add** and subtract numbers. We studied shapes such as **circles** and squares. We even **learned** how to **weigh** things and to measure **height**. I will never forget Ms. Simmons's **lessons**.

1. Ms. Simmons was the writer's homeroom teacher. _____

2. Ms. Simmons was scary, but her lessons were wonderful. _____

3. The students only learned how to add numbers. _____

4. The writer will remember Ms. Simmons's lessons forever. _____

67

1 branch
[bræntʃ]

n. a part of a tree that grows from the trunk
on the branch
→ A bird is sitting on the **branch**.

2 breath
[breθ]
v. breathe

n. the act of taking air in and out of the body
take a deep breath
→ Take a deep **breath** and try to relax.

3 chance
[tʃæns]

n. the possibility of something happening
good chance
→ The player missed a good **chance** to score a goal.

4 clear
[kliər]

adj. easy to see or understand   (syn) clean   (ant) dark
clear sky
→ There is a **clear** sky with no clouds today.

5 control
[kəntróul]

v. to limit something or make something happen
n. the act of limiting something
control an area → The soldiers **control** the area.
in control → The pilot is in **control** of the plane.

6 create
[kriéit]
adj. creative

v. to make something new   (ant) destroy
create a monster
→ Dr. Frankenstein **created** a monster.

7 dry
[drai]

adj. having no water   (ant) wet
v. to remove the water from something
dry season → The **dry** season in Africa lasts for six months.
dry one's hair → **Dry** your hair with this towel.

8 earth
[ɜːrθ]

n. the planet that we live on (usually Earth); the ground
live on the Earth
→ Dinosaurs lived on the **Earth** a long time ago.

9 factory
[fǽktəri]

n. a place where people make things
car factory
→ His father works in a car **factory**.

10 garbage
[gáːrbidʒ]

n. anything useless that will be thrown away   (syn) trash
garbage can
→ Don't put food waste in the **garbage** can.

11 important
[impɔ́ːrtənt]

adj. of great value or necessary

important role

→ Vitamins play an **important** role in our bodies.

12 jungle
[dʒʌ́ŋgl]

n. a forest with many plants in a hot, wet place

king of the jungle

→ The lion is the king of the **jungle**.

13 leaf
[liːf]

n. a flat green part of a plant

maple leaf

→ Maple **leaves** change colors in fall.

14 nature
[néitʃər]

adj. natural

n. all the animals, plants, and things not made by people   *syn* environment

beauty of nature

→ The poet admired the beauty of **nature**.

15 pond
[pɑnd]

n. a small area of still water

fish pond

→ There is a small fish **pond** in the garden.

16 shade
[ʃeid]

n. a dark place that does not get the sun's direct light   *syn* shadow

in the shade

→ The cows are resting in the **shade**.

17 silent
[sáilənt]

adj. making little or no noise   *syn* quiet   *ant* loud

keep silent

→ Please keep **silent** during class.

18 storm
[stɔːrm]

n. bad weather with heavy rain and strong winds

heavy storm

→ Our flight was canceled because of the heavy **storm**.

19 weather
[wéðər]

n. outdoor conditions in the air such as rain or temperature

weather forecast

→ The **weather** forecast says it will snow.

20 yard
[jɑːrd]

n. a small area of land with grass around a house

front yard

→ His house has a large front **yard**.

A **Circle the words that fit the definitions.**

1. to limit something or make something happen

   a. dry   b. breath   c. create   d. control

2. bad weather with heavy rain and strong winds

   a. storm   b. garbage   c. shade   d. nature

3. the possibility of something happening

   a. factory   b. chance   c. earth   d. leaf

4. the planet that we live on

   a. branch   b. pond   c. weather   d. earth

5. a part of a tree that grows from the trunk

   a. jungle   b. garbage   c. branch   d. yard

B **Circle the two words in each group that are opposites.**

1. a. silent   b. loud   c. important   d. shade

2. a. important   b. earth   c. clear   d. dark

3. a. breath   b. destroy   c. create   d. control

4. a. wet   b. leaf   c. jungle   d. dry

C **Circle the words that best fit the sentences.**

1. Animals like tigers live in jungles | ponds .

2. The workers at that earth | factory make automobiles.

3. Take a deep chance | breath and calm down.

4. The dogs are playing in the weather | yard right now.

5. Nature | Storm is beautiful in this area during spring.

6. The weather | garbage in the jungle is usually hot and wet.

D Choose the correct words to complete the sentences.

1. They have lots of fish living in their _____.
   a. shade   b. branch   c. pond   d. breath

2. Please put all of this _____ in the trash can.
   a. chance   b. storm   c. factory   d. garbage

3. It is always cooler in the _____ than in the sun.
   a. shade   b. leaf   c. weather   d. control

4. It is _____ for students to have a dream.
   a. silent   b. important   c. clear   d. dry

5. She picked a _____ from the tree to look at it more closely.
   a. leaf   b. yard   c. nature   d. jungle

E Read the passage. Then, fill in the blanks.

These days, the **Earth** is suffering from pollution. Everything is polluted. As a result, the **weather** has changed. Some places do not get rain, so they have become **dry**. Other places get a lot of **storms**. Many **factories** send **garbage** into the air. So it is hard to see the **clear** sky. Many people cannot get a single **breath** of fresh air. **Jungles** and **ponds** are also polluted. It is hard to see birds on tree **branches** and fish in **ponds**.

We should do something to help polluted **nature**. For example, we can clean up **garbage** in **ponds** and **jungles**. **Factories** should **create** less **garbage**. We can plant more trees to help make **clear** skies. It is **important** to protect **nature** for the future.

1. The _____ has changed because of pollution.

2. The sky is not _____ because of garbage in the air.

3. People should clean up polluted _____.

4. We need to plant trees and _____ less garbage.

1	**alone**
	[əlóun]
		adj. apart from others
		adv. by oneself
		    be alone ➡ He likes to be **alone** on the weekend.
		    live alone ➡ Shrek lived **alone** in the deep forest.	

2	**birth**
	[bɜːrθ]
	v. bear
		n. the act of being born
		    give birth to
		    ➡ She gave **birth** to a son last night.	

3	**cousin**
	[kʌ́zən]
		n. a child of one's aunt or uncle
		    younger cousin
		    ➡ I have to take care of my younger **cousin** this weekend.

4	**daughter**
	[dɔ́ːtər]
		n. the female child of a mother or father (ant) son
		    only daughter
		    ➡ Mina is the only **daughter** of her parents.	

5	**elderly**
	[éldərli]
		adj. very old (ant) young
		    elderly man
		    ➡ He offered his seat to an **elderly** man.

6	**forget**
	[fərgét]
	forget - forgot -
	forgotten
		v. not to be able to remember something (ant) remember
		    forget to do
		    ➡ Don't **forget** to do your homework by tomorrow.

7	**friendship**
	[fréndʃip]
		n. a good relationship between friends
		    start a friendship
		    ➡ They started their **friendship** in kindergarten.	

8	**future**
	[fjúːtʃər]
		n. a time that will come later (ant) past
		    near future
		    ➡ I will travel abroad in the near **future**.

9	**lovely**
	[lʌ́vli]
		adj. beautiful; very pleasant (syn) pretty (ant) ugly
		    lovely eyes
		    ➡ The little girl has **lovely** eyes.

10	**meal**
	[miːl]
		n. food served at breakfast, lunch, or dinner
		    big meal
		    ➡ Lunch is my big **meal** of the day.	

11 ordinary
[ɔ́:rdənèri]

adj. usual and not special

ordinary people
→ It's a story about **ordinary** people.

12 parent
[pé(:)ərənt]

n. a child's mother or father

good parent
→ It is difficult to become a good **parent**.

13 past
[pæst]

n. time gone by   (ant) future
adj. relating to time gone by

in the past → Their problems happened in the **past**.
past event → We still remember the **past** event.

14 raise
[reiz]

v. to move something to a higher place; to care for a child or animal   (syn) lift

raise one's hand → **Raise** your hand if you know the answer.
raise a child → The country is good for **raising** a child.

15 son
[sʌn]

n. the male child of a mother or father   (ant) daughter

the oldest son
→ Tom is the oldest **son** in his family.

16 task
[tæsk]

n. work that somebody has to do

difficult task
→ Her boss gave her a difficult **task**.

17 vacation
[veikéiʃən]

n. a period of time when a school is closed

go on vacation
→ I plan to go on **vacation** next week.

18 watch
[wɑtʃ]

n. a clock one wears on the wrist
v. to look at something for a time

wear a watch → He wears a **watch** on his left arm.
watch a movie → Let's **watch** a movie this Saturday.

19 wise
[waiz]
n. wisdom

adj. able to make good choices and decisions   (syn) clever

wise decision
→ You should make a **wise** decision for the future.

20 wonderful
[wʌ́ndərfəl]

adj. extremely good   (ant) terrible

wonderful day
→ Have a **wonderful** day.

A   **Circle the correct definitions for the given words.**

1. ordinary
   a. very pleasant
   c. relating to time gone by
   b. extremely good
   d. usual and not special

2. watch
   a. not to be able to remember something
   c. to care for a child or animal
   b. to look at something for a time
   d. do move something to a higher place

3. birth
   a. the act of being born
   c. a time that will come later
   b. a period of time when a school is closed
   d. a child of one's aunt or uncle

4. alone
   a. very old
   c. apart from others
   b. relating to time gone by
   d. beautiful

B   **Circle the two words in each group that are opposites.**

1. a. future   b. vacation   c. past   d. parent

2. a. daughter   b. meal   c. task   d. son

3. a. watch   b. forget   c. raise   d. remember

4. a. past   b. alone   c. wonderful   d. terrible

C   **Circle the words that best fit the sentences.**

1. Simon has a close task | friendship with David.

2. A wise | past man knows a lot of things.

3. It can be difficult to raise | birth a child.

4. Where will we go on watch | vacation this winter?

5. The weather is so lovely | wise after it rains.

6. Every parent | future is welcome to attend the school festival.

D **Choose the correct words to complete the sentences.**

1. Try to complete your _____ by 5:00.
   a. births   b. friendships   c. tasks   d. sons

2. Nobody knows what will happen in the _____.
   a. future   b. past   c. parent   d. cousin

3. They will meet their _____ this weekend.
   a. cousins   b. watches   c. friendships   d. futures

4. I sometimes eat a snack between _____.
   a. daughters   b. meals   c. sons   d. vacations

5. My grandparents are _____, but they are still active.
   a. past   b. wonderful   c. lovely   d. elderly

E **Read the passage. Then, write T for true or F for false.**

Jenny's **parents** say, "We're going on **vacation**." "Are we visiting the beach? I want to go swimming," Jenny asks. "We're going to see your **cousin** Mary. She gave **birth** to a baby **daughter** recently," her mother answers.

Jenny is unhappy because she wants to go on a beach trip. But when she sees Mary's **daughter**, she **forgets** about that. The baby is so **lovely**, and Jenny enjoys **watching** the baby. She loves holding the baby, too.

Jenny's **parents** help Mary a lot. They cook **meals** for her. They clean the house. They take care of Mary's **son**, too. At the end of the trip, Jenny does not want to leave. It was not an **ordinary** trip. But it was a **wonderful** one.

1. Jenny and her family go to the beach on vacation.   _____

2. Jenny thinks Mary's baby son is lovely.   _____

3. Jenny's parents take care of Mary and her family.   _____

4. Jenny spends a great time at her cousin's house.   _____

A Choose and write the correct words for the definitions.

factory	impossible	straight	pity
shade	forgive	gather	raise

1. to feel sorry for someone ➡ _____

2. to move something to a higher place ➡ _____

3. without a bend or curve ➡ _____

4. a dark place that does not get the sun's direct light ➡ _____

5. unable to be done or to happen ➡ _____

6. to stop being upset with a person who has hurt one ➡ _____

7. a place where people make things ➡ _____

8. to bring together in one place ➡ _____

B Circle the words that are the most similar to the underlined words.

1. She is wearing a <u>pretty</u> gold necklace.
   a. lovely   b. ordinary   c. wise   d. elderly

2. At school, students <u>study</u> subjects like history and science.
   a. count   b. add   c. weigh   d. learn

3. Please <u>carry</u> your books to class every day.
   a. bring   b. attend   c. gather   d. accept

4. Tommy is always <u>quiet</u> during class.
   a. impossible   b. dry   c. silent   d. important

5. The general gave a <u>sign</u> to the soldiers.
   a. character   b. signal   c. speed   d. limit

C **Choose the correct forms of the words to complete the sentences.**

1. It is important to communicate | communication well with others.

2. Old people sometimes have a lot of wise | wisdom .

3. How much does your dog weigh | weight ?

4. Many people use | useful the Internet to find information.

5. He loves to creative | create stories for his children.

D **Complete the sentences with the words in the box.**

1. We looked in the room, but it was _____.

2. Kate looks _____, but she has a unique talent.

3. Alice won the contest and got a _____.

4. It rained all night long during the _____.

5. I will _____ the package to you this afternoon.

ordinary

deliver

prize

empty

storm

E **Write the correct phrases in the blanks.**

| weather forecast | circle the answers | board game |
| forget to do | gather together | top speed |

1. You should _____ within 30 minutes.

2. Many people will _____ at the gym.

3. Do not _____ your homework tonight.

4. The car's _____ is 200 kilometers per hour.

5. According to the _____, tomorrow will be cloudy.

6. The children will play a _____ after school.

77

F **Circle the mistakes. Then, write the correct sentences.**

1. You should make a choose soon.

➡ _____

2. The building is more than 50 meters height.

➡ _____

3. They enjoy spending a lot of time in natural.

➡ _____

4. The teach always asks the students many questions.

➡ _____

5. She had an accident in a past.

➡ _____

G **Complete the crossword puzzle.**

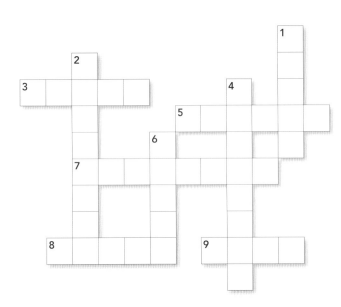

Across

3. something done out of kindness

5. the possibility of something happening

7. a chart showing the days, weeks, and months of a year

8. to give lessons to students at a school

9. a small area of still water

Down

1. to find two things that are the same

2. to succeed in dealing with a problem

4. a period of time when a school is closed

6. to measure how heavy or light something is

H **Read the passage. Then, answer the questions below.**

Solving Problems Together

Around the world, there are many problems. Bad **weather** and high **temperatures** cause problems for farmers. People are cutting down trees in **jungles**. There is **garbage** in lots of places. And **factories** and cars are **creating** pollution. So it is hard for people to **breathe** in some places.

Sometimes things look bad. But these problems are not **impossible** to **overcome**. People can work **together** to solve these problems.

There are many **tasks** people can do. People can recycle things. Some people can **spend** time cleaning up **garbage**. Other people are busy, so they **donate** money to help others. Some **wise** men hold meetings. Then, they give **lessons** on solving problems. **Ordinary** people can **attend** them and **learn useful** information. If people try hard **together**, they can make the **future** better.

1. What is the passage mainly about?
   a. some big problems in jungles
   b. a group that helps people
   c. the importance of recycling
   d. how people are solving problems

2. Which is NOT true about the problems?
   a. Many trees are cut down in jungles.
   b. We can see garbage in a lot of places.
   c. Factories try to reduce pollution.
   d. Cars are a cause of pollution.

3. Which is NOT a task people can do?
   a. farm more land
   b. recycle things
   c. donate money to others
   d. give other people lessons

4. What is causing problems for farmers?

   ➡ _____

5. How can people solve these problems?

   ➡ _____

1	**address** [ədrés]	*n.* the place where a person or building is located home address → What is your home **address**?
2	**classical** [klǽsikəl]	*adj.* traditional in form, style, or idea; related to music using various instruments *syn* ancient classical ballet → She is the master of **classical** ballet. classical music → He often performs **classical** music.
3	**company** [kʌ́mpəni]	*n.* an organization that sells goods or services　　*syn* business computer company → Microsoft is a very large computer **company**.
4	**court** [kɔːrt]	*n.* a place where judges work to follow the law Supreme Court → Nobody can challenge the decisions of the Supreme **Court**.
5	**dentist** [déntist]	*n.* a person who treats people's teeth visit the dentist → I will visit the **dentist** after school.
6	**design** [dizáin]	*n.* a drawing or plan of something *v.* to make a drawing or plan of something basic design → The basic **design** of a car is very simple. design a car → Her job is to **design** cars.
7	**director** [diréktər]	*n.* a person in charge of making a film movie director → The movie **director** won an award.
8	**fashion** [fǽʃən] *adj.* fashionable	*n.* a popular style of clothing or hair latest fashion → The actress is dressed in the latest **fashion**.
9	**food** [fuːd]	*n.* anything that people or animals eat or drink　　*syn* diet eat food → All humans must eat **food** to survive.
10	**judge** [dʒʌdʒ]	*n.* a person who makes decisions in a court of law *v.* to form an opinion about something state judge → Mr. Whitson works as a state **judge**. judge a book → Don't **judge** a book by its cover.

11 language
[lǽŋgwidʒ]

n. a system of communication used by people
second language
→ We learn English as a second **language**.

12 library
[láibrèri]

n. a building with books that people can read or borrow
visit a library
→ He will visit the **library** to do some research.

13 mayor
[méiər]

n. the elected leader of a city or town
elect a mayor
→ The city will elect a new **mayor** on Wednesday.

14 plan
[plæn]

n. a method or idea for doing something
v. to think of a method or idea for doing something
have plans → Do you have any **plans** for this weekend?
plan ahead → We need to **plan** ahead for the festival.

15 police
[pəlíːs]

n. a group of people who make sure everyone follows the law
call the police
→ In an emergency, you should call the **police**.

16 public
[pʌ́blik]

adj. open to all the people in a community   (ant) private
public library
→ Is there a **public** library near here?

17 recommend
[rèkəménd]

v. to say that something is good or useful   (syn) suggest
recommend a book
→ Can you **recommend** a good book for teenagers?

18 speech
[spiːtʃ]
v. speak

n. a talk given by a person to a group of listeners
attend a speech
→ I will attend a **speech** by a Nobel Prize winner.

19 therefore
[ðéərfɔ̀ːr]

adv. as a result
and therefore
→ He often tells lies and **therefore** has few friends.

20 uniform
[júːnifɔ̀ːrm]

n. a special set of clothes for school or work
wear a uniform
→ All the students at that school wear a **uniform**.

A **Match the words with their definitions.**

1. recommend •   • a. to say that something is good or useful

2. court •   • b. to form an opinion about something

3. judge •   • c. a popular style of clothing or hair

4. fashion •   • d. traditional in form, style, or idea

5. director •   • e. a place where judges work to follow the law

6. classical •   • f. the elected leader of a city or town

7. mayor •   • g. a person in charge of making a film

8. public •   • h. open to all the people in a community

B **Circle the two words in each group that have the same meaning.**

1. a. address   b. business   c. company   d. language

2. a. food   b. diet   c. director   d. speech

3. a. design   b. suggest   c. judge   d. recommend

4. a. classical   b. public   c. ancient   d. therefore

C **Circle the words that best fit the sentences.**

1. The fashion | judge listened to the case in court.

2. Please let me know your mailing address | director .

3. Be sure to wear your speech | uniform to school.

4. She is able to speak three foreign designs | languages .

5. The mayor made a wonderful speech | police last night.

6. I will borrow some books from the library | fashion .

D **Choose the correct words to complete the sentences.**

1. The owner is pleased with the _____ of the building.
   a. design   b. court   c. speech   d. uniform

2. There will be an election for the _____ of the city tomorrow.
   a. company   b. library   c. address   d. mayor

3. My tooth hurts, so I need to see a _____.
   a. director   b. judge   c. dentist   d. police

4. We _____ need to work hard all the time.
   a. classical   b. therefore   c. public   d. speech

5. Try to _____ for the future, and then you will be successful.
   a. judge   b. public   c. recommend   d. plan

E **Read the passage. Then, fill in the blanks.**

This morning, the principal makes a **speech**. "There are no classes today," she says. "Today is career day. **Therefore**, you will learn about different jobs."

The students visit one classroom. Some **police** are there. The **police** tell the students about their jobs. Then, the students visit another classroom. They see a **dentist**. He shows how to check people's teeth. The students are happy to learn from him. The students also learn about other jobs. They meet a **judge**, a **fashion** designer, and a **language** teacher. The **mayor** talks to them. A musician plays some **classical** music for them. A librarian talks about working in a **library**.

At the end of the day, the students are tired but happy. Some start making **plans** for their future careers.

1. The principal makes a _____ to the students.

2. The students meet some _____ in the first classroom.

3. The _____ shows the students how to check teeth.

4. The students learn about working in a _____.

83

1	**beside** [bisáid]	*prep.* at the side of something (syn) next to beside someone → Who is the lady standing **beside** Sarah?
2	**blow** [blou] blow - blew - blown	*v.* to send air out from the mouth; to move like the wind blow out a candle → Cindy **blew** out the candles on the cake. blow hard → A cold wind is **blowing** hard from the north.
3	**bug** [bʌg]	*n.* an insect big bug → There is a big **bug** on the floor.
4	**climb** [klaim] *n.* climber	*v.* to go up something toward the top climb a mountain → He usually **climbs** mountains on the weekend.
5	**danger** [déindʒər] *adj.* dangerous	*n.* the chance that one might be hurt or killed (ant) safety in danger → The ship is in **danger** due to the storm.
6	**flood** [flʌd]	*n.* a large amount of water that covers an area *v.* for water to rise above its normal level major flood → The hurricane caused a major **flood**. flood a city → The rising waters **flooded** the city.
7	**giant** [dʒáiənt]	*adj.* very tall or large (ant) tiny *n.* a very tall or large man or monster giant animal → An elephant is a **giant** animal. become a giant → He grew up to become a **giant**.
8	**grand** [grænd]	*adj.* impressive in size or appearance (syn) amazing grand hotel → The view of the **grand** hotel is wonderful.
9	**hill** [hil]	*n.* an area of land higher than the land around it top of a hill → Our car climbed slowly to the top of the **hill**.
10	**hunt** [hʌnt]	*v.* to find animals to kill for food *n.* the act of finding animals to kill for food hunt alone → Animals like snakes often **hunt** alone. fox hunt → The men are going on a fox **hunt**.

11 mud
[mʌd]

n. wet and soft earth

in the mud

→ The pig loves to play in the **mud**.

12 ocean
[óuʃən]

n. a large body of salt water   `syn` sea

sail on the ocean

→ The ship is sailing on the **ocean**.

13 reach
[riːtʃ]

v. to stretch a hand toward something; to arrive somewhere

reach for   → He **reached** for the ball and caught it.

reach an airport   → We **reached** the airport on time.

14 recycle
[riːsáikl]

v. to prepare materials in order to use them again   `syn` reuse

recycle plastic

→ We should **recycle** plastic to help the environment.

15 remove
[rimúːv]

v. to take something away   `syn` get rid of

remove a box

→ She **removed** the box from her room.

16 rock
[rɑk]

n. a large stone on the ground

big rock

→ Some people are climbing up the big **rock**.

17 shadow
[ʃǽdou]

n. an area of darkness created when light is blocked   `syn` shade

cast a shadow

→ The tree cast a **shadow** on the lake.

18 solar
[sóulər]

adj. relating to the sun

solar power

→ They heat their house with **solar** power.

19 tiny
[táini]

adj. very small   `syn` little   `ant` huge

tiny boy

→ The **tiny** boy grew up and became an adult.

20 wonder
[wʌ́ndər]

v. to think about something; to be surprised

n. something strange or surprising

wonder about   → I often **wonder** about my old friends.

look in wonder   → They looked in **wonder** at the waterfall.

A   **Circle the words that fit the definitions.**

1. to send air out from the mouth

   a. hunt   b. climb   c. reach   d. blow

2. a large amount of water that covers an area

   a. bug   b. flood   c. danger   d. hill

3. wet and soft earth

   a. ocean   b. shadow   c. mud   d. rock

4. very tall or large

   a. giant   b. solar   c. tiny   d. grand

5. to think about something

   a. remove   b. flood   c. wonder   d. recycle

B   **Write S for synonym or A for antonym next to each pair of words.**

1. _____ recycle – reuse   2. _____ danger – safety

3. _____ giant – tiny   4. _____ ocean – sea

5. _____ grand – amazing   6. _____ tiny – huge

C   **Circle the words that best fit the sentences.**

1. The woman beside | solar my mother is my aunt.

2. Can you hunt | reach the box on the top shelf?

3. We will have a picnic on top of the ocean | hill .

4. There are too many bugs | giants like ants in the house.

5. Some tiny | grand animals are hard to see.

6. They will break the mud | rock into very small stones.

D Choose the correct words to complete the sentences.

1. You must _____ the stairs up to the second floor.

    a. wonder   b. recycle   c. flood   d. climb

2. _____ power is very cheap and clean energy.

    a. Solar   b. Tiny   c. Grand   d. Giant

3. Please _____ my name from the membership list.

    a. blow   b. remove   c. climb   d. wonder

4. The men like to _____ deer and ducks in winter.

    a. hunt   b. recycle   c. blow   d. flood

5. On a sunny day, you can see your _____ on the ground.

    a. danger   b. ocean   c. rock   d. shadow

E Read the passage. Then, write T for true or F for false.

A man is walking through the jungle. He was with some other people. But he got lost. He **wonders** where they are. He sits on a **rock** and thinks. Suddenly, the man believes something is wrong. He senses **danger**.

He looks at a tall tree and sees a **giant shadow**. **Beside** the tree is a tiger. The tiger is **hunting** him. The man runs, but the tiger chases him. He quickly **reaches** a river. He dives into the river and starts swimming. The tiger does not follow him, so he is safe.

The man stays near the river. He walks for days. Many **bugs** bite him. So he covers his body with **mud**. Finally, he **reaches** the **ocean**. A ship comes by and saves him.

1. The man sits on a rock with some other people. _____

2. There is a tiger beside a tree. _____

3. The tiger follows the man into the river. _____

4. The man reaches the ocean and gets saved. _____

1 among
[əmʌ́ŋ]

prep. in the middle of something
among friends
→ Mark is the tallest boy **among** my friends.

2 best
[best]

adj. of the highest quality or excellence   (ant) worst
n. something or someone of higher quality than others
best player → Rick is the **best** player on our team.
do one's best → You should do your **best** on the test.

3 complain
[kəmpléin]

v. to say that one is unhappy about something
complain about
→ Stop **complaining** about your homework.

4 event
[ivént]

n. something that happens, especially something important
annual event
→ The school festival is an annual **event**.

5 excited
[iksáitid]
v. excite

adj. very happy or pleased   (ant) bored
get excited
→ He got **excited** when he saw the superstar.

6 guide
[gaid]

v. to lead others to a certain place
n. a person who leads others to certain places
guide a group → She **guided** a group through the museum.
tour guide → The tour **guide** knows a lot about London.

7 hurt
[hɜːrt]
hurt - hurt - hurt

v. to cause physical pain
hurt oneself
→ You will **hurt** yourself if you are not careful.

8 lead
[liːd]
n. leader
lead - led - led

v. to go before others to show them the way   (syn) guide   (ant) follow
lead the way
→ The guide is **leading** the way to the gallery.

9 lonely
[lóunli]

adj. feeling bad or sad because one is alone   (syn) alone
feel lonely
→ The girl felt **lonely** without any friends to play with.

10 present
[prézənt]

n. something one person gives to another   (syn) gift
adj. happening now
birthday present → Thank you for your birthday **present**.
present time → He is out at the **present** time.

11 punish
[pʌ́niʃ]

v. to make someone suffer for doing something bad
punish a student
→ The teacher **punished** the student for lying.

12 receive
[risíːv]

v. to get something from another person   (syn) accept   (ant) give
receive a present
→ Did you **receive** any presents on your birthday?

13 social
[sóuʃəl]
n. society

adj. relating to relations with others
social problem
→ Pollution is becoming a **social** problem.

14 sure
[ʃuər]
adv. surely

adj. certain that something is true or will happen   (syn) confident
make sure
→ Make **sure** you turn off the lights.

15 treat
[triːt]

n. something special that one person does for another
v. to behave in a certain way toward a person
special treat → He gave his dog a special **treat**.
treat like a child → My parents **treat** me like a child.

16 trust
[trʌst]

v. to believe a person
n. the act of believing a person
trust each other → We should **trust** each other.
gain one's trust → He finally gained her **trust**.

17 understand
[ʌ̀ndərstǽnd]
understand - understood - understood

v. to know what someone or something means
understand a rule
→ I can't **understand** the rules of the game.

18 virtual
[vɜ́ːrtʃuəl]

adj. almost the same as described; created by a computer   (ant) real
virtual reality
→ **Virtual** reality games are becoming popular.

19 wave
[weiv]

v. to move one's hand from side to side in greeting
n. a line of moving water
wave goodbye → She **waved** goodbye to her parents.
huge wave → The huge **wave** made the ship sink.

20 write
[rait]
n. writer
write - wrote - written

v. to make words or numbers with a pen or a pencil
write a letter
→ She often **writes** letters to her grandparents.

A Circle the correct definitions for the given words.

1. excited

　　a. in the middle of something　　　　b. very happy or pleased

　　c. happening now　　　　　　　　　　d. created by a computer

2. trust

　　a. to believe a person　　　　　　　b. to lead others to a certain place

　　c. to cause physical pain　　　　　　d. to get something from another person

3. wave

　　a. the act of believing a person　　　b. something one person gives to another

　　c. a line of moving water　　　　　　d. a person who leads others to certain places

4. virtual

　　a. relating to relations with others　　b. feeling bad or sad because one is alone

　　c. of the highest quality or excellence　d. almost the same as described

B Circle the two words in each group that have the same meaning.

1. a. hurt　　　　b. accept　　　　c. treat　　　　d. receive

2. a. present　　b. gift　　　　　c. event　　　　d. trust

3. a. virtual　　b. social　　　　c. lonely　　　　d. alone

4. a. lead　　　b. punish　　　　c. guide　　　　d. understand

C Circle the words that best fit the sentences.

1. Joe is among | sure the smartest students at the school.

2. She does not punish | understand how to answer the question.

3. I hurt | led myself when I fell on the floor.

4. Amy is the virtual | best writer in the writing club.

5. Are you sure | social this is the correct answer?

6. You should not treat | write your sister so poorly.

D **Choose the correct words to complete the sentences.**

1. Mary _____ that she had too many chores.

   a. received   b. led   c. treated   d. complained

2. Can you _____ us to Central Park, please?

   a. trust   b. guide   c. wave   d. hurt

3. Jack was _____ for being late for school.

   a. punished   b. led   c. understood   d. trusted

4. John has a busy _____ life since he has lots of friends.

   a. best   b. lonely   c. virtual   d. social

5. Please _____ your name at the top of the paper.

   a. hurt   b. receive   c. write   d. wave

E **Read the passage. Then, fill in the blanks.**

Some animals live alone. However, humans are **social** animals. So we like living **among** other people. We feel **lonely** without others. Having relationships with others helps humans very much.

   The family is an important **social** unit. Parents and their children live together. Parents help their children very much. They **guide** their children through the early parts of their lives. Parents teach their children to read and **write**. They make **sure** their children **understand** many things. They sometimes give **presents** to their children. However, parents also sometimes **punish** their children for doing bad things.

   Some children **complain** about their parents. They say their parents don't **treat** them well. But children should **understand** that most parents do their **best**. They want to be **sure** their children have great lives.

1. An important _____ unit for humans is the family.

2. Parents make _____ their children can read and write.

3. Parents may have to _____ bad children.

4. Children may _____ that their parents don't treat them well.

1	**believe** [bilíːv]	*v.* to think that something is true (syn) trust believe in ghosts → Do you **believe** in ghosts?
2	**cheer** [tʃiər] *adj.* cheerful	*v.* to shout loudly to encourage someone *n.* a shout of joy or support cheer loudly → The fans are **cheering** loudly for their team. big cheer → The audience gave a big **cheer** for the player.
3	**confident** [kánfidənt]	*adj.* sure of one's ability to do well and to be successful confident attitude → Her **confident** attitude helps her do well.
4	**cry** [krai]	*v.* to have tears coming from one's eyes; to call out (ant) laugh cry loudly → The baby sometimes **cries** loudly.
5	**effect** [ifékt]	*n.* something that happens due to another thing (syn) result bad effect → Television has a bad **effect** on children.
6	**handsome** [hǽnsəm]	*adj.* good looking (ant) ugly handsome face → All people remember his **handsome** face.
7	**heavy** [hévi]	*adj.* weighing a lot (ant) light heavy backpack → Joe is carrying a **heavy** backpack.
8	**helpful** [hélpfl]	*adj.* providing aid to others helpful advice → Thank you for your **helpful** advice.
9	**honest** [ánist] *n.* honesty	*adj.* telling the truth and not cheating honest person → An **honest** person doesn't lie.
10	**listen** [lísn]	*v.* to pay attention to or try to hear a sound listen carefully → Everyone **listened** carefully to the teacher.

11 main
[mein]

adj. biggest in size or importance

main idea

→ What is the **main** idea of the story?

---

12 pain
[pein]

n. a feeling of hurt

in pain

→ The boy screamed loudly in **pain**.

---

13 perfect
[pɜ́ːrfikt]

adj. having no problems ⓢⓨⓝ complete

perfect score

→ Dave got a **perfect** score on his test.

---

14 proud
[praud]

adv. proudly

adj. satisfied about doing something

be proud of

→ She was **proud** of winning a prize.

---

15 scary
[ské(ː)əri]

adj. making people afraid

scary movie

→ We watched a **scary** movie last night.

---

16 secret
[síːkrət]

adj. kept hidden from others ⓢⓨⓝ unknown

n. something that is kept hidden from others

secret place → He hides his treasure in a **secret** place.

keep a secret → Can you keep a **secret**?

---

17 serious
[sí(ː)əriəs]

adj. very bad or dangerous

serious mistake

→ I made a **serious** mistake on the test.

---

18 shape
[ʃeip]

n. the outer form of something

special shape

→ The building has a special **shape**.

---

19 upset
[ʌpsét]

adj. very sad or unhappy about something ⓢⓨⓝ worried ⓐⓝⓣ glad

v. to make someone feel unhappy

look upset → You look terribly **upset** today.

upset someone → The bad weather **upset** everyone in the room.

---

20 weak
[wiːk]

adj. not having much energy or strength ⓐⓝⓣ strong

feel weak

→ Her legs felt **weak** after a long walk.

A **Match the words with their definitions.**

1. believe •   • a. telling the truth and not cheating

2. confident •   • b. biggest in size or importance

3. effect •   • c. kept hidden from others

4. honest •   • d. sure of one's ability to do well and to be successful

5. main •   • e. to shout loudly to encourage someone

6. secret •   • f. to think that something is true

7. proud •   • g. satisfied about doing something

8. cheer •   • h. something that happens due to another thing

B **Circle the two words in each group that are opposites.**

1. a. handsome   b. helpful   c. ugly   d. honest

2. a. confident   b. perfect   c. heavy   d. light

3. a. weak   b. upset   c. glad   d. helpful

4. a. strong   b. main   c. proud   d. weak

C **Circle the words that best fit the sentences.**

1. My parents always give me helpful | handsome advice.

2. She likes to believe | listen to the radio at night.

3. Do you like main | scary stories about ghosts?

4. The clock on the wall is in the shape | pain of a diamond.

5. Let me tell you John's secret | cheer right now.

6. Her legs are too upset | weak to walk a long way.

D **Choose the correct words to complete the sentences.**

1. He is _____ because he hurt his arm.
   a. upsetting   b. listening   c. crying   d. believing

2. Tell the dentist about the _____ in your tooth.
   a. shape   b. secret   c. cheer   d. pain

3. The weather is _____ to go on a picnic.
   a. perfect   b. weak   c. scary   d. handsome

4. The airplane has a _____ problem, so it can't take off.
   a. proud   b. confident   c. honest   d. serious

5. Karen will play the _____ character in the movie.
   a. upset   b. main   c. heavy   d. effect

E **Read the passage. Then, write T for true or F for false.**

Most people want others to like them. There is a **secret** to doing that. You need a good personality and appearance.
   It is important to be **honest**. You should be **confident**, too. Others want to be friends with people who **listen** well. And nobody likes unhappy people. Happy people are much more fun. It is better to be a **helpful** person. And don't have many **secrets**. You need to help **weak** people, too. A person's appearance is important. Not everyone can be **handsome** or pretty. But people can do their best to look good. They can exercise to get in good **shape**.
   So do your best to improve your personality and appearance. Be **proud** of yourself, and people will **cheer** for your success.

1. People should be honest and confident to be liked. _____

2. Nobody likes happy and helpful people. _____

3. People can exercise to look handsome. _____

4. People can improve their personalities by trying hard. _____

1	**bend** [bend] bend - bent - bent	*v.* to change the shape of something bend one's back → **Bend** your back and touch your toes.
2	**care** [keər] *adj.* careful	*n.* a worry or concern *v.* to be worried or concerned about something with care → Please move the box with **care**. care about → You really **care** about your health.
3	**catch** [kætʃ] catch - caught - caught	*v.* to grab, often after chasing something catch a train → He ran quickly to **catch** the train.
4	**deep** [di:p]	*adj.* going down far from the top deep water → Be careful about swimming in **deep** water.
5	**disease** [dizí:z]	*n.* something that causes people or animals to get sick syn illness cure a disease → Doctors hope to cure the **disease** soon.
6	**failure** [féiljər] *v.* fail	*n.* a lack of success at doing something syn mistake ant success end in failure → All our efforts ended in **failure**.
7	**happen** [hǽpən]	*v.* to take place syn occur happen suddenly → The earthquake **happened** suddenly.
8	**headache** [hédèik]	*n.* pain in the head bad headache → My mom often suffers from bad **headaches**.
9	**health** [helθ] *adj.* healthy	*n.* the condition of one's body in good health → My grandpa is 80 and still in good **health**.
10	**look** [luk]	*v.* to watch something; to search for something syn see *n.* the act of watching something look at → He **looked** at me and smiled. take a look → Please take a **look** at my report.

96

11 lose
[luːz]
lose - lost - lost

v. to be unable to find something; to fail to win a game   *syn* forget
lose a key → Please do not **lose** the key.
lose a game → We **lost** the game to our rival.

12 possible
[pásəbl]

adj. able to happen   *ant* impossible
possible solution
→ I'm thinking of a **possible** solution to the problem.

13 powerful
[páuərfəl]

adj. able to affect people and events   *syn* strong   *ant* weak
powerful man
→ He is one of the most **powerful** men in the world.

14 seem
[siːm]

v. to appear to be something or to have a particular quality
seem like
→ She **seems** like a good student.

15 stretch
[stretʃ]

v. to extend one's body parts as much as possible; to make something longer by pulling on it
stretch one's hand → He **stretched** his hand toward the top shelf.
stretch a rubber band → **Stretch** a rubber band by pulling on it.

16 trouble
[trʌbl]

n. a problem or difficulty
v. to cause a problem or difficulty   *syn* worry
in trouble → You are going to be in big **trouble**.
trouble someone → I don't want to **trouble** you.

17 use
[juːz][juːs]
adj. useful

v. to do something with a machine or skill
n. the act of using something
use electricity → The heater **uses** a lot of electricity.
in use → The old computer is still in **use** now.

18 voice
[vɔis]

n. the sounds a person makes while speaking
quiet voice
→ Speak in a quiet **voice** in the library.

19 warn
[wɔːrn]
n. warning

v. to tell someone about a danger or problem
warn someone
→ My mother **warned** me not to cheat.

20 wash
[wɑʃ]

v. to remove dirt by using water
wash one's hand
→ **Wash** your hands with soap and water.

A Circle the words that fit the definitions.

1. to be worried or concerned about something

   a. bend   b. catch   c. care   d. look

2. the condition of one's body

   a. disease   b. headache   c. trouble   d. health

3. to tell someone about a danger or problem

   a. happen   b. warn   c. lose   d. stretch

4. the sounds a person makes while speaking

   a. voice   b. failure   c. look   d. use

5. going down far from the top

   a. possible   b. powerful   c. seem   d. deep

B Write S for synonym or A for antonym next to each pair of words.

1. _____ disease – illness   2. _____ failure – success

3. _____ look – see   4. _____ lose – forget

5. _____ trouble – worry   6. _____ powerful – weak

C Circle the words that best fit the sentences.

1. Bend | Look the plastic straw to drink the soda.

2. A snowstorm will warn | happen later today.

3. It is possible | deep to take a break for a while.

4. It seems | stretches likely to rain today.

5. Lewis can wash | use a computer very well.

6. He threw a rock into the deep | powerful hole.

D **Choose the correct words to complete the sentences.**

1. The boys will try to _____ some fish at the pond.
  a. catch   b. warn   c. lose   d. happen

2. I got a _____ from all the loud noise.
  a. failure   b. health   c. headache   d. voice

3. _____ your arms and legs before you go into the water.
  a. Use   b. Warn   c. Catch   d. Stretch

4. You need to _____ your dirty hands right now.
  a. happen   b. wash   c. seem   d. bend

5. Tina got in _____ for breaking the window.
  a. trouble   b. failure   c. voice   d. look

E **Read the passage. Then, fill in the blanks.**

Doctors take **care** of sick people. For example, they help people with **headaches** and colds. They also assist people with **diseases** like cancer. They help these people have good **health** again.

However, it is **possible** to prevent sicknesses and **diseases**. There are several things people can do to avoid **catching** colds or getting sick. First, people can **wash** their hands regularly. This will kill harmful germs. Next, people can **care** for their bodies. They should eat healthy food and exercise.

Finally, people should **look** out for **trouble**. When they think something is wrong with their bodies, they should see a doctor. The doctor can **warn** them about any danger. That can keep them from getting sick. So it is **possible** to have good **health**.

1. Doctors help people with _____ like cancer.

2. People can avoid _____ colds by washing their hands.

3. People should look out for _____ in their bodies.

4. Doctors can warn people to help them have good _____.

A   Choose and write the correct words for the definitions.

main	lose	public	voice
treat	giant	classical	wave

1. related to music using various instruments ➡ _____

2. biggest in size or importance ➡ _____

3. open to all the people in a community ➡ _____

4. to behave in a certain way toward a person ➡ _____

5. to fail to win a game ➡ _____

6. to move one's hand from side to side in greeting ➡ _____

7. the sounds a person makes while speaking ➡ _____

8. very tall or large ➡ _____

B   Circle the words that are the most similar to the underlined words.

1. Tom's father is the president of a small <u>business</u>.

   a. address   b. uniform   c. library   d. company

2. People don't <u>trust</u> the shepherd boy anymore.

   a. cheer   b. upset   c. believe   d. listen

3. Something bad might <u>occur</u> if you are not careful.

   a. bend   b. stretch   c. happen   d. seem

4. Jane is <u>confident</u> she can do well on the history test.

   a. sure   b. virtual   c. excited   d. lonely

5. Please <u>get rid of</u> all of this garbage in here.

   a. recycle   b. remove   c. blow   d. hunt

C **Choose the correct forms of the words to complete the sentences.**

1. Eat lots of vegetables in order to have good health | healthy .

2. The mountain climb | climber is going up Mount Everest.

3. Harry is one of the most cheer | cheerful people at school.

4. The fans are so excite | excited about tonight's game.

5. I can't wait to hear Mr. Dawson speak | speech tonight.

D **Complete the sentences with the words in the box.**

1. Please _____ a good dish on the menu for me.

2. The accident had a bad _____ on her life.

3. He _____ how he could finish the work on time.

4. He is one of the most _____ men in the world.

5. Joy _____ a phone call from her grandparents.

> effect
>
> received
>
> powerful
>
> recommend
>
> wondered

E **Write the correct phrases in the blanks.**

| lead the way | waved goodbye | perfect score |
| deep water | movie director | tiny boy |

1. The _____ is working on a drama now.

2. Please _____, or I will get lost.

3. Fish like sharks often live in _____.

4. My younger brother is such a _____.

5. No students got a _____, but one got a 99.

6. The actor _____ to the people in the theater.

101

F   **Circle the mistakes. Then, write the correct sentences.**

1. She hopes to work in the fashionable industry someday.

   ➡ _____

2. It took many years to create an advanced social.

   ➡ _____

3. Please be care when you are climbing the mountain.

   ➡ _____

4. John very proud accepted the prize.

   ➡ _____

5. Snakes can be very danger animals.

   ➡ _____

G   **Complete the crossword puzzle.**

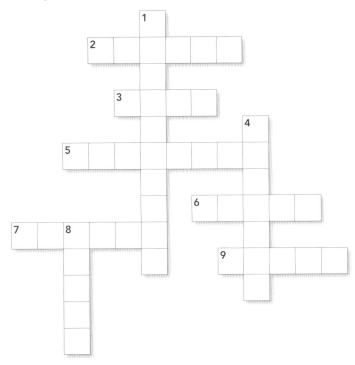

Across

2. telling the truth and not cheating
3. to change the shape of something
5. able to happen
6. the elected leader of a city or town
7. a drawing or plan of something
9. a large amount of water that covers an area

Down

1. to know what someone or something means
4. to prepare materials in order to use them again
8. making people afraid

H Read the passage. Then, answer the questions below.

A School Visitor

One day at school, a **handsome** man arrives. The students are **excited**. He is the owner of a big **company** and a very **powerful** man. He will make a **speech** today. When the man stands up, the students **cheer**.

Then, he talks about his life. When he was young, he was **tiny** and **weak**. He did not like school. He didn't **listen** in class and always **complained**. He caused **trouble**, so his teachers **punished** him.

One day, his father got a **disease**. The man made a promise. If his father's **health** would improve, he would change. His father got better. So the man changed. He worked hard and started a **design company**. He earned a lot of money and became a **helpful** person. Now everyone is **proud** of him.

1. What is the passage mainly about?
   a. a man's life story   b. a speech
   c. a design company   d. a man's father

2. How was the man when he was young?
   a. handsome and powerful   b. sad and sick
   c. tiny and weak   d. rich and helpful

3. What happened to the man's father?
   a. He started a company.
   b. He got better.
   c. He became rich.
   d. He worked hard.

4. What will the man do at the school today?
   ➡ _____

5. How did the man earn a lot of money?
   ➡ _____

1	**agree** [əgríː] *n.* agreement	*v.* to think the same as another person ant disagree agree with → I **agree** with your opinion.
2	**along** [əlɔ́(ː)ŋ]	*prep.* moving on or beside something along a road → They are walking **along** the road now.
3	**become** [bikʌ́m] become - became - become	*v.* to turn or change into something become a doctor → His parents want him to **become** a doctor.
4	**chat** [tʃæt]	*v.* to talk in a friendly way *n.* a friendly talk syn conversation chat with → Jenny is **chatting** with her friend. short chat → I had a short **chat** with Tom.
5	**contact** [kántækt]	*v.* to communicate with a person *n.* the act of communicating with someone contact by email → I **contact** my old friends by email. keep in contact with → Bill and I keep in **contact** with each other.
6	**dream** [driːm]	*n.* images in one's mind while sleeping; a goal syn hope *v.* to have images in one's mind while sleeping have a dream → He had a bad **dream** last night. dream of → I have always **dreamed** of going abroad.
7	**drink** [driŋk] drink - drank - drunk	*v.* to take a liquid into the body *n.* any liquid a person can put into the body drink water → It's important to **drink** water every day. soft drink → Soft **drinks** are bad for your teeth.
8	**famous** [féiməs]	*adj.* well known to many people ant unknown famous actress → That woman is a **famous** actress.
9	**follow** [fálou]	*v.* to go after a person or thing follow a road → **Follow** the road for ten kilometers.
10	**hope** [houp]	*v.* to have a wish for the future *n.* the act of wishing for the future hope to win → I **hope** to win a gold medal. hope of → They have no **hope** of success.

11 keep
[kiːp]
keep - kept - kept

v. to stay in a particular condition without changing
keep silent
→ The teacher told the students to **keep** silent.

12 lend
[lend]

v. to let someone have or use something for a while   [ant] borrow
lend a book
→ The public library **lends** books to people.

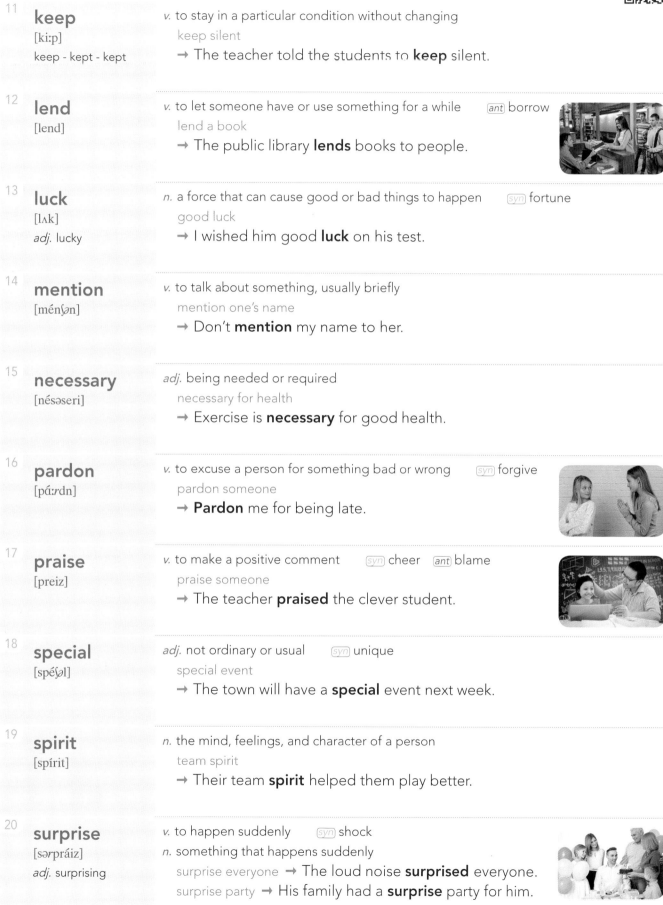

13 luck
[lʌk]
adj. lucky

n. a force that can cause good or bad things to happen   [syn] fortune
good luck
→ I wished him good **luck** on his test.

14 mention
[ménʃən]

v. to talk about something, usually briefly
mention one's name
→ Don't **mention** my name to her.

15 necessary
[nésəseri]

adj. being needed or required
necessary for health
→ Exercise is **necessary** for good health.

16 pardon
[páːrdn]

v. to excuse a person for something bad or wrong   [syn] forgive
pardon someone
→ **Pardon** me for being late.

17 praise
[preiz]

v. to make a positive comment   [syn] cheer   [ant] blame
praise someone
→ The teacher **praised** the clever student.

18 special
[spéʃəl]

adj. not ordinary or usual   [syn] unique
special event
→ The town will have a **special** event next week.

19 spirit
[spírit]

n. the mind, feelings, and character of a person
team spirit
→ Their team **spirit** helped them play better.

20 surprise
[sərpráiz]
adj. surprising

v. to happen suddenly   [syn] shock
n. something that happens suddenly
surprise everyone → The loud noise **surprised** everyone.
surprise party → His family had a **surprise** party for him.

A **Match the words with their definitions.**

1. chat •   • a. the act of wishing for the future

2. famous •   • b. the mind, feelings, and character of a person

3. hope •   • c. to talk in a friendly way

4. mention •   • d. to happen suddenly

5. necessary •   • e. to communicate with a person

6. surprise •   • f. well known to many people

7. spirit •   • g. to talk about something, usually briefly

8. contact •   • h. being needed or required

B **Choose and write the correct words for the blanks.**

special	praise	agree	lend	luck	pardon

1. forgive   = _____   2. borrow ≠ _____

3. fortune   = _____   4. blame   ≠ _____

5. disagree ≠ _____   6. unique = _____

C **Circle the words that best fit the sentences.**

1. The road goes follow | along the river.

2. The teacher became | praised angry at the rude student.

3. Susan had a spirit | dream about her family last night.

4. John agreed | drank to meet Tom at the theater at eight.

5. Let's buy a contact | special present for Rose for her birthday.

6. The team hoped | surprised us by winning the game.

D **Choose the correct words to complete the sentences.**

1. Mark was thirsty, so he asked for a _____.

    a. spirit   b. drink   c. luck   d. pardon

2. The dog is _____ its owner down the street.

    a. following   b. mentioning   c. dreaming   d. becoming

3. You had better _____ quiet during the film.

    a. surprise   b. lend   c. agree   d. keep

4. The baseball player became _____ around the world.

    a. chat   b. necessary   c. famous   d. along

5. Dave's mother _____ he does well on the test.

    a. contacts   b. lends   c. hopes   d. becomes

E **Read the passage. Then, write T for true or F for false.**

Everyone needs friends. People need friends to **chat** with. They need friends to share their **dreams** and **hopes** with, too.

Friends do many things for one another. Friends **praise** others when they do something good. They **pardon** their friends when they do something bad. They **lend** their friends things they need. And on **special** occasions, they **surprise** their friends with presents.

Would you like to **become** a good friend? It is easy. Try to **chat** with your friends. **Mention** the things you are interested in. And listen to them talk about other things. **Agree** to go out with your friends when you have time. **Contact** them regularly to ask how they are doing. With **luck**, you will have a lot of close friends.

1. People chat with their friends and tell them their dreams. _____

2. Friends pardon others when they do something good. _____

3. You can be a good friend by listening to people. _____

4. Do not agree to go out with your friends. _____

1 **buy**
[bai]
buy - bought - bought

v. to pay money for something   (ant) sell
buy a car
→ My mother will **buy** a new car this weekend.

2 **cheap**
[tʃiːp]

adj. costing little money   (ant) expensive
cheap price
→ She bought the bag for a **cheap** price.

3 **delicious**
[dilíʃəs]

adj. tasting very good   (syn) tasty
delicious meal
→ Thank you for the **delicious** meal.

4 **different**
[dífərənt]
n. difference

adj. not like something else
look different
→ The twins look **different** from each other.

5 **dinosaur**
[dáinəsɔːr]

n. a large animal that lived millions of years ago
dinosaur bones
→ The scientist discovered some **dinosaur** bones.

6 **emperor**
[émpərər]

n. the ruler of an empire
Roman emperor
→ The Roman **emperor** ruled a large area of land.

7 **far**
[faːr]

adj./adv. not close to something   (ant) near
far from → My house is not **far** from the library.
far away → The man drove **far** away from his home.

8 **free**
[friː]
n. freedom

adj./adv. able to do what one wants; costing no money
free time → What do you usually do in your **free** time?
for free → The elderly can ride on buses for **free**.

9 **global**
[glóubəl]

adj. relating to the whole world   (syn) international
global market
→ Their products are popular on the **global** market.

10 **interesting**
[íntrəstiŋ]
n. interest

adj. able to hold people's attention   (syn) exciting   (ant) boring
interesting place
→ Egypt is an **interesting** place to visit.

11 map
[mæp]

n. a detailed picture of an area of land
map of Asia
→ They are looking at a **map** of Asia.

12 paint
[peint]
n. painting

n. a colored liquid that can be put on another surface
v. to create a picture with paint   (syn) draw
white paint → She prefers white **paint** on the wall.
paint a picture → Michelangelo **painted** many beautiful pictures.

13 plane
[plein]

n. a machine with wings that can fly   (syn) airplane
fly on a plane
→ We will fly on a **plane** to Italy.

14 point
[pɔint]

v. to show something by using one's finger
n. an idea or thought
point at → It is rude to **point** at people.
good point → Mary made a good **point** in her report.

15 reason
[ríːzən]

n. the cause of an action or belief
good reason
→ Do you have a good **reason** for being late?

16 ride
[raid]
ride - rode - ridden

v. to go somewhere in a vehicle
n. the act of going somewhere in a vehicle
ride one's bike → Tom usually **rides** his bike to school.
give a ride → Can you give me a **ride**?

17 shine
[ʃain]
adj. shiny

v. to create or reflect light
shine brightly
→ The sun is **shining** brightly today.

18 statue
[stǽtʃuː]

n. an image that is made of stone, wood, or metal   (syn) sculpture
the Statue of Liberty
→ The **Statue** of Liberty is in New York.

19 want
[wɑnt]

v. to hope or wish for something
want to know
→ Why do you **want** to know the reason?

20 wide
[waid]

adj. very long from one side to the other   (ant) narrow
wide area
→ The city covers a **wide** area of land.

A   Circle the correct definitions for the given words.

1. different

    a. not like something else

    b. costing little money

    c. not close to something

    d. able to do what one wants

2. map

    a. an idea or thought

    b. the ruler of an empire

    c. the cause of an action or belief

    d. a detailed picture of an area of land

3. shine

    a. to pay money for something

    b. to go somewhere in a vehicle

    c. to create or reflect light

    d. to hope or wish for something

4. global

    a. tasting very good

    b. relating to the whole world

    c. able to hold people's attention

    d. costing no money

B   Circle the two words in each group that are opposites.

1. a. sell   b. paint   c. point   d. buy

2. a. far   b. expensive   c. cheap   d. wide

3 a. global   b. delicious   c. interesting   d. boring

4. a. narrow   b. wide   c. different   d. free

C   Circle the words that best fit the sentences.

1. My mother's apple pie always tastes delicious | free .

2. How far | wide is Seoul from Paris?

3. The teacher bought | pointed at the blackboard.

4. Can you please give me a ride | plane home today?

5. Susan gave a good statue | reason for forgetting her homework.

6. We will see the bones of maps | dinosaurs at the museum.

D **Choose the correct words to complete the sentences.**

1. He became the _____ when his father died.
  a. map   b. plane   c. emperor   d. reason

2. If you buy one item, you will get another one for _____.
  a. global   b. free   c. far   d. delicious

3. The artist likes to _____ pictures of forests.
  a. shine   b. ride   c. point   d. paint

4. There is a large _____ of a dragon in front of the building.
  a. statue   b. dinosaur   c. plane   d. reason

5. Jason _____ to take a trip to Europe this summer.
  a. buys   b. shines   c. wants   d. points

E **Read the passage. Then, fill in the blanks.**

The students at Central Elementary School visit a museum. In front of the museum, there are many **statues**. The students think the **statues** are **interesting**.

Then, they go inside. There is a museum **map** on the wall. The **map** shows all exhibits in the museum. There are many **interesting** exhibits today. Some students **want** to see an exhibit about **dinosaurs**. Others **want** to see an exhibit about **planes**. There is also an exhibit about a Chinese **emperor**.

The students go to **different** exhibits. They **point** at some of the **interesting** items. At lunch, they get together for a **delicious** lunch. Some of them visit the gift shop and **buy** some items. They are not **cheap**. But each student gets a **free** postcard from the museum.

1. The _____ in front of the museum are interesting.

2. Inside the museum, the students look at a _____ on the wall.

3. There are exhibits about dinosaurs and a Chinese _____.

4. The museum gives each student a postcard for _____.

1	**bone** [boun]	*n.* one of the body's hard parts that form a frame in it break a bone → Jason fell and broke a **bone** in his hand.	
2	**carry** [kǽri]	*v.* to take something from one place to another (syn) bring carry a bag → Dan is **carrying** a heavy bag over his shoulder.	
3	**cross** [krɔ(:)s]	*v.* to go from one side to the other cross a road → Wait for a green light to **cross** the road.	
4	**cure** [kjuər]	*v.* to make an illness go away cure a patient → The doctor hopes to **cure** the patient.	
5	**example** [igzǽmpl]	*n.* something explaining or supporting a statement (syn) instance for example → For **example**, birds lay eggs.	
6	**face** [feis]	*n.* the front of the head from the forehead to the chin round face → She has a round **face** and small eyes.	
7	**finger** [fíŋgər]	*n.* one of the five ending parts of each hand snap one's fingers → He snapped his **fingers** at his friend.	
8	**float** [flout]	*v.* to move slowly on the surface of the water (ant) sink float on water → Plastic bottles are **floating** on the water.	
9	**human** [hjú:mən]	*n.* a person *adj.* relating to people human race → The **human** race has billions of people. human body → The **human** body is very mysterious.	
10	**hurry** [hʌ́ri]	*v.* to do something very quickly hurry up → You should **hurry** up to take the train.	

11 knee
[niː]

n. the part of the body connecting the upper and lower leg

hurt one's knee

→ I hurt my **knee** while playing soccer.

12 medicine
[médisn]
adj. medical

n. something that a person takes to cure an illness   syn drug

take medicine

→ Take this **medicine** three times a day.

13 narrow
[nǽrou]

adj. not long from one side to the other   syn thin   ant wide

narrow street

→ The car is driving down the **narrow** street.

14 pull
[pul]

v. to move something toward oneself   ant push

pull open

→ You should **pull** open the door.

15 push
[puʃ]

v. to move something away from oneself   ant pull

push someone

→ The bully **pushed** the boy to the ground.

16 respond
[rispánd]

v. to answer   syn reply

respond to

→ She **responded** to my question very quickly.

17 sweat
[swet]

v. to have water come from one's body
n. water that comes from one's body

sweat a lot → She **sweats** a lot when she jogs.
in a sweat → He woke up in a **sweat** at midnight.

18 thirsty
[θɜ́ːrsti]

adj. wanting or needing to drink something

feel thirsty

→ The weather was hot so I felt **thirsty**.

19 throat
[θrout]

n. the front part of a person's neck

sore throat

→ He had a sore **throat** and couldn't talk.

20 tongue
[tʌŋ]

n. the part of the mouth that helps people eat and taste

stick out one's tongue

→ Stick out your **tongue** and say, "Ahhh."

A **Circle the words that fit the definitions.**

1. to go from one side to the other

   a. carry   b. cure   c. cross   d. float

2. to do something very quickly

   a. pull   b. respond   c. sweat   d. hurry

3. water that comes from one's body

   a. sweat   b. face   c. human   d. medicine

4. wanting or needing to drink something

   a. narrow   b. thirsty   c. throat   d. finger

5. one of the body's hard parts that form a frame in it

   a. bone   b. human   c. tongue   d. knee

B **Write S for synonym or A for antonym next to each pair of words.**

1. _____ carry – bring   2. _____ float – sink

3. _____ medicine – drug   4. _____ narrow – thin

5. _____ push – pull   6. _____ respond – reply

C **Circle the words that best fit the sentences.**

1. The teacher gives the students many examples | faces in class.

2. You have five knees | fingers on each hand.

3. I took some medicine because of my sore sweat | throat .

4. We use our bone | tongue to taste food.

5. She was thirsty | narrow , so she got a drink.

6. Please respond | float when I ask you a question.

D **Choose the correct words to complete the sentences.**

1. This medicine will be helpful to _____ your cold.
   a. hurry　　　　b. carry　　　　c. push　　　　d. cure

2. Wash your _____ and brush your teeth.
   a. bone　　　　b. face　　　　c. medicine　　　　d. human

3. All _____ have two eyes and two ears.
   a. humans　　　　b. tongues　　　　c. examples　　　　d. knees

4. He fell down and hurt his _____.
   a. example　　　　b. sweat　　　　c. knee　　　　d. medicine

5. You must _____ the door to make it open.
   a. sweat　　　　b. push　　　　c. respond　　　　d. float

E **Read the passage. Then, write T for true or F for false.**

Do you want to be a doctor? If you want to be a doctor, you must learn many things. First, you must learn about **humans** and body parts like **knees** and **fingers**. You need to learn about **bones**. And you need to know what **medicine** to give sick people.

After becoming a doctor, you have to remember many things about diseases. For **example**, a patient may visit you. She says she is **thirsty** and her **throat** hurts. You must **hurry** to figure out her problem. You might look at her **tongue**. You might ask her if her **face** hurts or if she is **sweating**. The patient will **respond** to you. After that, you can give her **medicine** to **cure** her. Doctors' work is hard but important.

1. Doctors need to learn about the human body. _____

2. Sick people know what medicine they need. _____

3. Doctors must hurry to figure out patients' problems. _____

4. Doctors do not need to ask patients any questions. _____

1 boil
[bɔil]
v. to heat water until it starts to become a gas (ant) freeze
boil water
→ First, **boil** some water to make spaghetti.

2 bottle
[bátl]
n. a glass or plastic container used for liquids
a bottle of water
→ He drank a **bottle** of water after jogging.

3 bowl
[boul]
n. a deep, round dish for holding food or a liquid
salad bowl
→ Put all the vegetables in the large salad **bowl**.

4 candle
[kǽndl]
n. a stick of wax that a person burns to create light
blow out a candle
→ Blow out the **candles** on the cake and make a wish.

5 dessert
[dizə́ːrt]
n. sweet food served at the end of a meal
favorite dessert
→ My favorite **dessert** is chocolate cake.

6 dictionary
[díkʃənəri]
n. a book that shows the meanings of words
in a dictionary
→ Check how to spell the word in a **dictionary**.

7 flat
[flæt]
adj. level with a surface (syn) even
flat roof
→ Many buildings in the town have **flat** roofs.

8 fresh
[freʃ]
adj. newly made or recently picked or caught (ant) old
fresh fruit
→ The local market sells **fresh** fruit and vegetables.

9 late
[leit]
adj. happening after an arranged or usual time (ant) early
adv. after a usual time
late summer → We had a lot of rain in **late** summer.
arrive late → Please do not arrive **late** for class.

10 light
[lait]
adj. weighing very little (ant) heavy
n. something that makes things bright
light in weight → Paper is very **light** in weight.
turn off a light → Turn off the **light** when you leave.

11 meat
[miːt]

n. the flesh of an animal that people eat

eat meat
→ Children should eat **meat** to get enough nutrients.

12 pattern
[pǽtərn]

n. a set of repeating lines, shapes, or colors   (syn) design

floral pattern
→ My sister is wearing a dress with a floral **pattern**.

13 pet
[pet]

n. an animal a person raises in a home
v. to touch an animal or a person gently

own a pet → Do you own a **pet**?
pet a dog → I like to **pet** my dog.

14 pick
[pik]

v. to make a choice; to take something with your fingers   (syn) choose

pick a number → **Pick** a number from one to ten.
pick a flower → Don't **pick** flowers in the garden.

15 roof
[ru(ː)f]

n. the top of a house or building

on the roof
→ There is a lot of snow on the **roof**.

16 sink
[siŋk]

sink - sank - sunk

v. to disappear below the surface of the water
n. a place in a kitchen or bathroom where water can flow

sink to the bottom → The ship is **sinking** to the bottom.
kitchen sink → Wash the dirty dishes in the kitchen **sink**.

17 spread
[spred]

spread - spread - spread

v. to extend something over a flat surface

spread a tablecloth
→ She **spread** a tablecloth over the table.

18 stair
[steər]

n. a set of steps leading to a different level

go up the stairs
→ Let's go up the **stairs** to the second floor.

19 wake
[weik]

adj. awake
wake - woke - woken

v. to get up; to make a person get up   (ant) sleep

wake up late → I usually **wake** up late on weekends.
wake someone up → My mom **wakes** me up each morning.

20 waste
[weist]

v. to use more of something than is necessary   (ant) save
n. garbage

waste time → Don't **waste** time watching TV.
household waste → Let's reduce our household **waste**.

A　**Match the words with their definitions.**

1. flat　•
2. light　•
3. dessert　•
4. pet　•
5. sink　•
6. spread　•
7. candle　•
8. meat　•

• a. sweet food served at the end of a meal
• b. to disappear below the surface of the water
• c. to extend something over a flat surface
• d. something that makes things bright
• e. a stick of wax that a person burns to create light
• f. level with a surface
• g. the flesh of an animal that people eat
• h. to touch an animal or a person gently

B　**Choose and write the correct words for the blanks.**

waste	late	wake	boil	pattern	pick

1. freeze ≠ _____
2. design = _____
3. sleep ≠ _____
4. early ≠ _____
5. save ≠ _____
6. choose = _____

C　**Circle the words that best fit the sentences.**

1. He wants to have a candle | bottle of juice.

2. He is fixing the pet | roof of my house.

3. Tom prefers the stairs | patterns to the elevator.

4. Let's boil | pick the water to cook the eggs.

5. A feather is late | light and not heavy.

6. The Earth doesn't have a flat | fresh surface.

D **Choose the correct words to complete the sentences.**

1. I was hungry, so I ate two _____ of rice.
   a. bowls   b. sinks   c. bottles   d. stairs

2. _____ fruits and vegetables are healthy foods.
   a. Light   b. Flat   c. Fresh   d. Late

3. You can use a _____ on the exam.
   a. dictionary   b. dessert   c. pet   d. meat

4. You should not _____ money on useless things.
   a. spread   b. waste   c. boil   d. wake

5. The bus came _____, so many people were waiting for it.
   a. flat   b. fresh   c. light   d. late

E **Read the passage. Then, fill in the blanks.**

On Saturday, Jennifer **wakes** up at 7:00. She does not have school today. But she has to do many chores.

First, she takes care of her **pet**. Choco, her dog, is hungry, so she gives him some **meat**. Next, she looks at the **sink**. There are all kinds of dirty **bowls**, plates, and **bottles** in it. She washes them all. After that, she is hungry, so she prepares a **light** breakfast of **fresh** fruit. She notices a **dictionary**, some **candles**, and some other things on the floor. So she **picks** them up and puts them away.

Finally, Jennifer leaves her home. She goes down the **stairs** and runs to the bus stop. She does not want to be **late** to meet her friend for lunch.

1. Jennifer _____ up early to do her chores.

2. Jennifer washes the dirty bowls, plates, and _____.

3. Jennifer eats a _____ breakfast of fresh fruit.

4. Jennifer runs so she will not be _____ for her meeting.

1 ask
[æsk]

v. to speak or write to someone to get information   *ant* answer
> ask a question
→ You can **ask** questions anytime.

2 block
[blɑk]

v. to stop someone from doing something
n. a solid piece of wood or stone with smooth sides
> block a road → A large rock is **blocking** the road.
> concrete block → The house is made of concrete **blocks**.

3 complete
[kəmplíːt]

v. to finish doing something   *syn* end   *ant* begin
adj. having everything
> complete one's homework → **Complete** your homework on time.
> complete series → I read the **complete** series in two weeks.

4 copy
[kápi]

v. to do or make something exactly like another
n. something exactly like another
> copy a picture → Can you **copy** the picture for me?
> make a copy → Please make a **copy** of this page.

5 enter
[éntər]
n. entrance

v. to go into a place; to start going to a school   *ant* exit
> enter a room → Before you **enter** the room, knock on the door.
> enter a college → He studied hard to **enter** the college.

6 exam
[igzǽm]

n. a test at a school
> take an exam
→ I will take a science **exam** tomorrow.

7 fail
[feil]
n. failure

v. not to be successful   *syn* lose   *ant* win
> fail an exam
→ Study hard, or you will **fail** the exam.

8 goal
[goul]

n. something that a person wants to achieve
> set a goal
→ Set a **goal** and make a plan.

9 grade
[greid]

n. a test or class score; a level in school
> good grade → Did you get a good **grade** in history?
> sixth grade → Jennifer is in the sixth **grade**.

10 hard
[hɑːrd]
adv. hardly

adj. difficult to do; solid and firm   *syn* tough   *ant* soft
adv. with great effort
> hard question → The teacher asks many **hard** questions.
> work hard → The students work **hard** to learn English.

11 manners
[mǽnəz]

n. behavior considered polite in a certain place
good manners
→ Parents teach their children to have good **manners**.

12 mean
[miːn]
mean - meant - meant

v. to have a particular meaning
adj. not nice   (ant) kind
mean to say → What do you **mean** to say?
mean boy → The **mean** boy makes fun of me.

13 pass
[pæs]

v. to throw something to another person; to be successful on a test
pass a ball → He **passed** the ball to his teammate.
pass a test → Study hard to **pass** the test.

14 poet
[póuit]

n. poem

n. a person who writes poems
well-known poet
→ Robert Browning was a well-known **poet** in England.

15 process
[práses]

n. a series of actions to achieve a result
difficult process
→ Learning a language is a difficult **process**.

16 record
[rikɔ́ːrd][rékərd]

v. to write something down to keep it for the future
n. a written account of something for the future
record the time → Please **record** the time you got up.
keep a record → Try to keep a **record** of everything.

17 result
[rizʌ́lt]

n. something that is caused by another thing   (syn) effect
good result
→ Your effort will have a good **result**.

18 right
[rait]

adj. true or correct   (ant) wrong
n. something that one is legally allowed to do
right answer → Tina got the **right** answer to the question.
human right → Freedom is a human **right**.

19 sentence
[séntəns]

n. a statement that has a subject and a verb
key sentence
→ Find the key **sentence** in this passage.

20 subject
[sʌ́bdʒekt]

n. something that is being discussed; a field of study
change a subject → We'd better change the **subject**.
favorite subject → What is your favorite **subject** at school?

A   **Circle the words that fit the definitions.**

1. something exactly like another

    a. goal   b. exam   c. copy   d. sentence

2. to go into a place

    a. enter   b. ask   c. fail   d. record

3. behavior considered polite in a certain place

    a. block   b. grade   c. process   d. manners

4. a person who writes poems

    a. record   b. poet   c. subject   d. result

5. true or correct

    a. complete   b. mean   c. right   d. hard

B   **Circle the two words in each group that have the same meaning.**

1. a. end   b. complete   c. block   d. enter

2. a. mean   b. fail   c. lose   d. record

3. a. tough   b. right   c. complete   d. hard

4. a. grade   b. goal   c. result   d. effect

C   **Circle the words that best fit the sentences.**

1. His grade | goal is to become a pilot one day.

2. That girl is so mean | manners to all of her friends.

3. Did you block | pass the science test last Friday?

4. Please record | fail all the information in a notebook.

5. The poet | subject of the talk is robots.

6. The math exam | copy was very hard, so I failed it.

D Choose the correct words to complete the sentences.

1. Jake often _____ strange questions in class.

   a. completes   b. blocks   c. fails   d. asks

2. My _____ on the math exam was a 85.

   a. grade   b. poet   c. subject   d. copy

3. Janet is in the _____ of learning French.

   a. copy   b. process   c. record   d. sentence

4. Write the answer by using ten short _____.

   a. sentences   b. manners   c. results   d. goals

5. Please do not _____ me from entering the room.

   a. mean   b. fail   c. block   d. complete

E Read the passage. Then, write T for true or F for false.

The students at Clearwater High School study **hard**. Their **goal** is to **enter** a good college. They study several **subjects** each day. They also learn good **manners** from their teachers.

When the students **enter** the school building, their learning starts. As a **result**, they must always be thinking. The teachers want the students to **ask** questions. **Asking** questions can help the students learn. Students should also **record** their thoughts in notebooks. That will help them learn to write good **sentences**. As a **result**, their writing skills will improve.

The students also have **exams**. Some students **pass** them, but others **fail** them. Then, they try again to get good **grades**. The **process** is not easy to achieve their **goals**, but the students do their best.

1. The students study one subject each day. _____

2. The teachers ask the students many questions. _____

3. The students write sentences about their thoughts. _____

4. The students do their best to achieve their goals. _____

A   **Choose and write the correct words for the definitions.**

complete	process	statue	spread
free	bone	narrow	become

1. not long from one side to the other   ➡ _____

2. to turn or change into something   ➡ _____

3. one of the body's hard parts that form a frame in it   ➡ _____

4. to extend something over a flat surface   ➡ _____

5. costing no money   ➡ _____

6. a series of actions to achieve a result   ➡ _____

7. an image that is made of stone, wood, or metal   ➡ _____

8. to finish doing something   ➡ _____

B   **Circle the words that are the most similar to the underlined words.**

1. The patient needs some powerful <u>drugs</u> to get better.

   a. bones   b. fingers   c. medicine   d. faces

2. The speech had a positive <u>effect</u> on many students.

   a. goal   b. exam   c. process   d. result

3. The meal at the restaurant last night was so <u>tasty</u>.

   a. delicious   b. wide   c. free   d. different

4. His mother told him to <u>choose</u> his birthday present.

   a. spread   b. sink   c. pick   d. wake

5. Lucy had a short <u>conversation</u> with her friend Kelly.

   a. surprise   b. chat   c. spirit   d. dream

C **Choose the correct forms of the words to complete the sentences.**

1. It is 10:00, but Janet is still not wake | awake .

2. The two men reached an agree | agreement late last night.

3. You must attend medical | medicine school to become a doctor.

4. We should enter | entrance the building from the front door.

5. The sun shines | shiny very brightly during the day.

D **Complete the sentences with the words in the box.**

1. My family bought a lovely cat at a _____ shop.

2. I _____ to take a break for a few minutes.

3. It is _____ for children to go to school.

4. Math is the most difficult _____ for me.

5. Please _____, or you will be late.

| subject |
| want |
| hurry |
| necessary |
| pet |

E **Write the correct phrases in the blanks.**

| good luck | make a copy | cheap price |
| cure the patient | failed the exam | waste time |

1. People believe that four-leaf clovers bring _____.

2. The doctor did his best to _____.

3. I would like to _____ of my ID card.

4. Please do not _____ before class starts.

5. She bought her bicycle for a _____.

6. Joe was shocked when he _____.

125

F **Circle the mistakes. Then, write the correct sentences.**

1. Mary's friends had a surprising party for her birthday.

   ➡ _____

2. He practiced a lot, so he will not failure the audition.

   ➡ _____

3. He does not believe in good or bad lucky.

   ➡ _____

4. You need to work hardly all the time.

   ➡ _____

5. The artist can painting pictures very well.

   ➡ _____

G **Complete the crossword puzzle.**

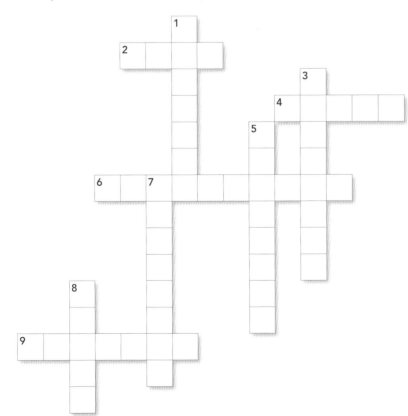

Across

2. the top of a house or building

4. relating to people

6. a book that shows the meanings of words

9. wanting or needing to drink something

Down

1. to communicate with a person

3. something that happens suddenly

5. a statement that has a subject and a verb

7. having everything

8. to show something by using one's finger

H Read the passage. Then, answer the questions below.

One Day in London

Tina and Jeff live **far** from London. One day, they **agree** to visit London together. They **want** to see many **famous** and **special** sights. They **ride** on a **plane** and fly there.

First, they visit a museum for **free**. They see many **interesting** things. They look at **dinosaur bones**, old **maps**, and **statues**. They **want** to **enter** one exhibit. But a guard **blocks** them. They need to pay for it.

After a while, they feel hungry and **thirsty**. They walked a lot, so their **knees** hurt, too. So they visit a drugstore to **buy** some **medicine**. After that, they go to a restaurant and order some food. It is not **cheap**, but it is **delicious**. They **buy** some **dessert**, too. Later, they walk on some **narrow** streets in London until **late** at night.

1. What is the passage mainly about?

  a. a visit to a museum

  b. dinner at a restaurant

  c. a trip to London

  d. the best places in London

2. How do Tina and Jeff go to London?

  a. by car   b. by ship

  c. by train   d. by plane

3. What do Tina and Jeff NOT see at the museum?

  a. paintings   b. old maps

  c. dinosaur bones   d. statues

4. Why do Tina and Jeff go to London?

  ➡ _____

5. What do Tina and Jeff do until late at night?

  ➡ _____

1　busy
[bízi]

adj. having a lot of things to do; full of people or vehicles

busy day → Mr. Smith had a **busy** day at work today.

busy place → The shopping center is a **busy** place around Christmas.

2　city
[síti]

n. a large and important town

large city

→ Busan is a large **city** in Korea.

3　coat
[kout]

n. clothing with long sleeves to keep people warm　(syn) jacket

put on one's coat

→ Put on your **coat** before you go out.

4　coin
[kɔin]

n. a piece of metal that people use as money

gold coin

→ The man buried gold **coins** in the ground.

5　expensive
[ikspénsiv]

adj. costing a lot of money　(ant) cheap

expensive picture

→ The *Mona Lisa* is the most **expensive** picture in the world.

6　fix
[fiks]

v. to make a broken thing work　(syn) repair　(ant) break

fix a bike

→ Dad **fixed** my broken bike.

7　fortune
[fɔ́:rtʃən]
adv. fortunately

n. luck; a large amount of money　(syn) wealth

good fortune → It was good **fortune** to pass the test.

make a fortune → He made a **fortune** by selling computers.

8　instead
[instéd]

adv. in place of someone or something

instead of

→ Let's stay home **instead** of going out.

9　junk
[dʒʌŋk]

n. something that is useless and nobody wants　(syn) garbage

junk food

→ You should not eat so much **junk** food.

10　minute
[mínit]

n. a period of time lasting sixty seconds

for a minute

→ Can I use your cell phone for a **minute**?

11 noon
[nuːn]

n. twelve o'clock in the middle of the day   (ant) midnight

    at noon
    → Most people usually eat lunch at **noon**.

12 pay
[pei]
pay - paid - paid

v. to spend money on something

    pay for
    → I'll **pay** for the movie tickets tonight.

13 quick
[kwik]
adv. quickly

adj. doing something fast   (ant) slow

    quick decision
    → You should make a **quick** decision about the plan.

14 sale
[seil]

n. the act of selling something; a time when items are sold at lower prices

    for sale → Sorry, but it's not for **sale**.
    on sale → All clothes at the store are on **sale**.

15 save
[seiv]
adj. safe

v. to keep a person away from danger; to keep to use later   (ant) spend

    save one's life → Thank you for **saving** my life.
    save money → She **saves** her money in a bank.

16 search
[sɜːrtʃ]

v. to look for something

    search for
    → **Search** for some information on the Internet.

17 slice
[slais]

v. to cut into pieces   (syn) divide
n. a thin and flat piece of food

    slice a cake → She **sliced** her birthday cake.
    slice of pizza → I ate three **slices** of pizza for lunch.

18 subway
[sʌ́bwèi]

n. an underground train in large cities

    subway station
    → Where is the **subway** station around here?

19 toy
[tɔi]

n. an object that people play with

    toy car
    → Tom wants a **toy** car for his birthday.

20 trade
[treid]

v. to exchange one thing for another

    trade goods
    → We want to **trade** many goods with foreign countries.

A **Circle the correct definitions for the given words.**

1. expensive

   a. doing something fast
   b. full of people or vehicles
   c. in place of someone or something
   d. costing a lot of money

2. minute

   a. a large and important town
   b. a period of time lasting sixty seconds
   c. a thin and flat piece of food
   d. a large amount of money

3. search

   a. to look for something
   b. to cut into pieces
   c. to keep a person away from danger
   d. to exchange one thing for another

4. sale

   a. an underground train in large cities
   b. an object that people play with
   c. the act of selling something
   d. luck

B **Write S for synonym or A for antonym next to each pair of words.**

1. _____ fix – break   2. _____ coat – jacket

3. _____ fortune – wealth   4. _____ noon – midnight

5. _____ slice – divide   6. _____ quick – slow

C **Circle the words that best fit the sentences.**

1. Most of Sue's family members live in the city | trade .

2. Instead | Busy of chicken, let's have fish for dinner.

3. People don't want coat | junk mail, so they block it.

4. I'm fixing | saving money to buy a new bike.

5. Mary bought a noon | toy for her son to play with.

6. Todd is very quick | expensive to learn foreign languages.

D **Choose the correct words to complete the sentences.**

1. Lisa was too _____ to help her sister.

    a. busy   b. expensive   c. instead   d. noon

2. Jeremy bought the chocolate with a few _____.

    a. slices   b. sales   c. coins   d. minutes

3. Mr. Taylor will _____ for everyone's lunch today.

    a. fix   b. pay   c. save   d. trade

4. You can go downtown fast by taking the _____.

    a. subway   b. toy   c. city   d. fortune

5. I will _____ you my cookies for your sandwich.

    a. search   b. save   c. slice   d. trade

E **Read the passage. Then, fill in the blanks.**

    Some people think good shoppers buy **expensive** items. But that is not true. You do not need to have a **fortune**. Instead, you can **pay** low prices.

    First, visit stores having **sales** to **save** money. Do not visit big **cities** to go shopping either. **Instead**, use the Internet and **search** for items online. You should be careful though. Many items for **sale** on the Internet are **junk**. So take your time when you are Internet shopping. Do not be **quick** to buy things. **Instead**, **search** slowly to buy good things for low prices. You can even **trade** for items you want sometimes.

    Those are some tips for shoppers. Remember not to pay **expensive** prices. Be smart, and you can buy great items for low prices.

1. Good shoppers do not have to buy _____ items.

2. Shoppers can _____ money by visiting stores having sales.

3. Be careful about buying items for _____ on the Internet.

4. Good shoppers _____ slowly to find low prices.

1 artist
[á:rtist]

n. a person who makes art
famous artist
→ Picasso was a famous **artist** during his life.

2 comic
[kámik]

n. a short story that is told through pictures
adj. funny   (syn) humorous
favorite comic → My favorite **comic** is *Garfield*.
comic show → Everyone laughed at the **comic** show.

3 correct
[kərékt]

adj. right and not wrong
v. to make something right
correct answer → Did she give the **correct** answer?
correct a mistake → **Correct** your mistakes again.

4 draw
[drɔ:]
draw - drew - drawn

v. to make a picture with a pen or pencil   (syn) paint
draw a picture
→ Her hobby is **drawing** pictures.

5 drive
[draiv]
drive - drove - driven

v. to make a vehicle move
drive a car
→ He will learn to **drive** a car next year.

6 film
[film]

n. a series of moving pictures with sound that people can watch
v. to make a movie
see a film → Let's see a **film** this weekend.
film a movie → They are **filming** a movie in Africa.

7 fly
[flai]
fly - flew - flown

v. to move through the air
fly from
→ We will **fly** from Seoul to Sydney next week.

8 hang
[hæŋ]
hang - hung - hung

v. to put something on a wall or ceiling
hang a picture
→ Let's **hang** the picture over here.

9 hero
[hí(:)ərou]

n. a person who does something brave or great   (syn) superhero
national hero
→ He became a national **hero** after the war.

10 horn
[hɔ:rn]

n. a hard, pointed growth on an animal's head; a musical instrument that sounds like a trumpet
sharp horn → Bulls use their sharp **horns** when they fight.
blow a horn → He is blowing a **horn** on the hill.

11 lift
[lift]

v. to move something to a higher place   ⓢⓎⓝ raise

lift a box

→ Can you **lift** the box by yourself?

---

12 loud
[laud]

adv. loudly

adj. making a lot of noise   ⓢⓎⓝ noisy   ⒶⓃⓉ silent

loud voice

→ Could you speak in a **loud** voice?

---

13 mix
[miks]

v. to combine two or more things

mix A and B

→ If you **mix** red and blue, you get purple.

---

14 science
[sáiəns]

adj. scientific

n. the study of nature and how things in it behave

study science

→ We study **science** at school.

---

15 skill
[skil]

n. the ability to do something well   ⓢⓎⓝ talent

computer skills

→ It is very useful to master computer **skills**.

---

16 strike
[straik]

strike - struck - struck

v. to hit something hard

strike one's foot

→ He **struck** his foot on the stone.

---

17 swim
[swim]

swim - swam - swum

v. to move in the water by using arms, legs, or fins

swim like a fish

→ Ted can **swim** like a fish.

---

18 talent
[tǽlənt]

adj. talented

n. the ability to do something well   ⓢⓎⓝ skill

unique talent

→ The child has a unique **talent** at music.

---

19 throw
[θrou]

v. to send an object through the air with a hand

throw a baseball

→ The pitcher can **throw** a baseball very fast.

---

20 win
[win]

n. winner

win - won - won

v. to finish first in a race; to get a prize for doing well   ⒶⓃⓉ lose

win a race   → Do you know who **won** the race?

win a gold medal   → She **won** a gold medal at the Olympics.

A   Match the words with their definitions.

1. artist   •   •   a. to send an object through the air with a hand

2. horn   •   •   b. a hard, pointed growth on an animal's head

3. loud   •   •   c. to make a movie

4. talent   •   •   d. making a lot of noise

5. throw   •   •   e. to combine two or more things

6. mix   •   •   f. a person who does something brave or great

7. hero   •   •   g. a person who makes art

8. film   •   •   h. the ability to do something well

B   Circle the two words in each group that have the same meaning.

1. a. correct   b. comic   c. humorous   d. loud

2. a. paint   b. drive   c. hang   d. draw

3. a. mix   b. win   c. lift   d. raise

4. a. talent   b. skill   c. science   d. horn

C   Circle the words that best fit the sentences.

1. The teacher corrects | mixes students when they are wrong.

2. Don't hang | drive so fast on the streets.

3. Strike | Throw the soccer ball with your foot.

4. She can swim | lift underwater for thirty seconds.

5. The school team drew | won the game by two goals.

6. I am interested in studying science | artist at school.

D **Choose the correct words to complete the sentences.**

1. Some birds like eagles can _____ high in the sky.
   a. fly   b. throw   c. drive   d. lift

2. The plants are _____ from the ceiling.
   a. winning   b. hanging   c. mixing   d. correcting

3. The strong man can _____ the heavy stone.
   a. swim   b. film   c. lift   d. fly

4. Find your _____ and get better at it.
   a. hero   b. artist   c. horn   d. talent

5. I cannot hear you because the music is too _____.
   a. correct   b. comic   c. skill   d. loud

E **Read the passage. Then, write T for true or F for false.**

   Everyone has different **talents**. Some people can **draw comics** well. Others have a **talent** for **swimming**. And many have other interesting **skills**.
   There is no **correct skill** or ability to have. Just try to develop the **skills** you have. For instance, maybe you like **science**. Study hard and learn to do it well. Or perhaps you are good at sports. Maybe you can **throw** a baseball very fast. Develop that **skill** and help your baseball team **win** games. Then, you can become a sports **hero**. Perhaps you love **films** or want to **fly** planes. Just try to develop your **talent**.
   Not everyone can be a great **artist**, ballplayer, or scientist. But everyone can have a wonderful life by developing their **talents**.

1. All people have the same talents.   _____

2. People should try to develop their skills.   _____

3. Everyone can become a sports hero.   _____

4. People's lives can be wonderful if they develop their talents.   _____

1 burn
[bɜːrn]

v. to heat something to make it catch on fire
  burn to the ground
  → The fire **burned** the house to the ground.

2 close
[klous][klouz]

adj. being near someone or something (ant) far
v. to shut a door, window, etc. (ant) open
  close to → My house is **close** to the library.
  close a door → Please **close** the door when you go out.

3 crash
[kræʃ]

v. to hit something, causing damage
  crash into
  → The truck **crashed** into a car.

4 drop
[drɑp]

v. to fall to the ground (ant) catch
  drop a plate
  → I **dropped** the plate, and it broke into pieces.

5 excuse
[ikskjúːs]

n. a reason for having done something bad or wrong
  make an excuse
  → Paul tried to make an **excuse** for being late.

6 fall
[fɔːl]
fall - fell - fallen

v. to go from a high position to a lower one (syn) drop (ant) rise
  fall down
  → She tripped and **fell** down.

7 final
[fáinəl]
adv. finally

adj. last in time, place, or order (ant) first
  final exam
  → He is studying for his **final** exams.

8 hold
[hould]
hold - held - held

v. to have in one's hands
  hold hands
  → The man and woman are **holding** hands.

9 jail
[dʒeil]

n. a place to keep people who did something bad (syn) prison
  go to jail
  → Jean Valjean went to **jail** for stealing bread.

10 mad
[mæd]

adj. very upset; crazy (syn) angry
  mad at → My mom is **mad** at me for telling a lie.
  go mad → He lost all his money and went **mad**.

| 11 | **sore**
[sɔːr] | *adj.* having pain in one's body
sore arm
→ He has a **sore** arm from throwing a baseball. |

| 12 | **spill**
[spil] | *v.* to pour a liquid out of a container by accident
spill milk
→ The boy **spilled** milk all over the floor. |

| 13 | **stress**
[stres] | *n.* pressure caused by difficulties in somebody's life
suffer from stress
→ My father suffers from **stress** at work. |

| 14 | **tear**
[teər]
tear - tore - torn | *v.* to pull something apart or into pieces
tear one's shirt
→ I **tore** my shirt on the tree. |

| 15 | **terrible**
[térəbl] | *adj.* very unpleasant; causing great harm   (syn) serious (ant) wonderful
terrible experience → The camp was a **terrible** experience for him.
terrible storm → A **terrible** storm hit the town last night. |

| 16 | **thief**
[θiːf] | *n.* a person who steals something
catch a thief
→ The police are trying to catch the **thief**. |

| 17 | **tired**
[taiərd]
v. tire | *adj.* wanting to rest or sleep
feel tired
→ He felt **tired** after driving a long distance. |

| 18 | **trick**
[trik] | *n.* an act to fool or cheat someone
v. to try to fool or cheat someone
play a trick → He always plays **tricks** on his friends.
trick someone → The boy **tricked** me on April Fools' Day. |

| 19 | **trip**
[trip] | *n.* the act of going to another place
v. to hit one's foot and then to fall down
take a trip → I plan to take a **trip** to Europe this summer.
trip on → I **tripped** on a book and fell down. |

| 20 | **yell**
[jel] | *v.* to say something in a very loud voice   (syn) shout
yell at
→ The teacher **yelled** at the sleeping student. |

A **Circle the words that fit the definitions.**

1. a place to keep people who did something bad
   a. stress   b. jail   c. thief   d. trip

2. to pull something apart or into pieces
   a. burn   b. close   c. hold   d. tear

3. a reason for having done something bad or wrong
   a. trick   b. trip   c. excuse   d. stress

4. wanting to rest or sleep
   a. tired   b. final   c. mad   d. sore

5. to say something in a very loud voice
   a. crash   b. spill   c. yell   d. trick

B **Circle the two words in each group that are opposites.**

1. a. far   b. sore   c. close   d. mad

2. a. yell   b. catch   c. drop   d. trick

3. a. burn   b. tear   c. rise   d. fall

4. a. first   b. final   c. tired   d. terrible

C **Circle the words that best fit the sentences.**

1. The fire dropped | burned the grass in the field.

2. Please hold | spill my phone for a moment.

3. He is taking medicine for his sore | mad throat.

4. Homework can cause jail | stress for some students.

5. It was the most terrible | final experience of his life.

6. Did you have a good time on your thief | trip ?

D Choose the correct words to complete the sentences.

1. The car _____ into a truck, so four people were hurt.

   a. spilled   b. held   c. closed   d. crashed

2. A _____ stole the money from the bank last night.

   a. thief   b. trip   c. trick   d. stress

3. You should not be so _____ at your parents.

   a. tired   b. final   c. sore   d. mad

4. He dropped the glass, and the water _____ out from it.

   a. tore   b. burned   c. spilled   d. yelled

5. The magician can do lots of magic _____.

   a. jails   b. tricks   c. trips   d. excuses

E Read the passage. Then, fill in the blanks.

Jeff was suffering from **stress** at work. He was **tired** of working. So he decided to take a **trip**. However, it was a big mistake. The **trip** was **terrible** and made him **mad**.

First, Jeff's plane departed late. When he arrived, he took a taxi to his hotel. But the driver **crashed** the car. Then, Jeff **dropped** his passport and lost it. At a restaurant, the chef **burned** Jeff's food. Finally, a **thief tricked** Jeff and stole all of his money. Jeff wanted the **thief** to go to **jail**. But the police could not find him.

Jeff got really **mad**. He **yelled** a lot, too. Then, he got a **sore** throat. He wanted to go home early. What a **terrible** trip!

1. Jeff took a trip because of his _____ at work.

2. Jeff's taxi driver _____ the car.

3. A _____ stole all of Jeff's money.

4. Jeff was really mad about his _____ trip.

1	**announce** [ənáuns]	*v.* to make a public statement about a plan or decision announce one's plans → She **announced** her plans to her family.
2	**central** [séntrəl] *n.* center	*adj.* in the middle of something central place → Hyde Park is located in a **central** place in the town.
3	**express** [iksprés] *n.* expression	*v.* to speak or write about a feeling or idea　(syn) communicate express one's opinion → You should **express** your opinion clearly.
4	**gate** [geit]	*n.* a door in a fence, wall, etc. open a gate → Do not open the **gate** at night.
5	**government** [gávərnmənt]	*n.* the group that controls a country or state strong government → They do not want a strong **government**.
6	**introduce** [ìntrədjúːs] *n.* introduction	*v.* to help two people meet each other introduce oneself → Let me **introduce** myself to you.
7	**life** [laif]	*n.* the state of being alive　(ant) death save one's life → The lifeguard at the pool saved her **life**.
8	**mall** [mɔːl]	*n.* a large building with a lot of shops　(syn) shopping center shopping mall → A new shopping **mall** will open in the center of town.
9	**message** [mésidʒ]	*n.* information given to another person　(syn) note leave a message → Would you like to leave a **message** for him?
10	**move** [muːv]	*v.* to change positions; to change the place where one lives move a chair → Could you **move** the chair to the kitchen? move to → Jane will **move** to a new city in July.

11 officer
[ɔ́(:)fisər]

n. someone in a position of authority in the army or government
police officer
→ She asked the police **officer** for help.

12 peace
[piːs]
adj. peaceful

n. a time of no war between countries or groups (ant) war
make peace
→ The UN tries to make **peace** between countries.

13 polite
[pəláit]

adj. having good manners and behaving properly (ant) rude
polite man
→ Mr. Johnson is a **polite** man and never gets angry.

14 rich
[ritʃ]

adj. having a lot of money or property (syn) wealthy (ant) poor
rich country
→ Singapore has become a **rich** country.

15 select
[silékt]

v. to choose one thing instead of another (syn) pick
select an answer
→ Think about the question and **select** an answer.

16 service
[sə́ːrvis]
v. serve

n. an act that someone does to help another
public service
→ The government tries to improve public **services**.

17 society
[səsáiəti]
adj. social

n. a group of people living together in a community
modern society
→ Pollution is a serious problem in modern **society**.

18 solve
[sɑlv]

v. to find the answer to the problem
solve a puzzle
→ Sarah is busy **solving** a puzzle.

19 structure
[strʌ́ktʃər]

n. something made from parts such as a bridge
strong structure
→ We want to build a strong **structure** in case of storms.

20 temple
[témpl]

n. a building used for the worship of a god or gods (syn) church
visit a temple
→ She visits the **temple** two times a week.

Unit 29 Exercise

A **Match the words with their definitions.**

1. central •   • a. to change the place where one lives

2. gate •   • b. having good manners and behaving properly

3. introduce •   • c. something made from parts such as a bridge

4. move •   • d. a door in a fence, wall, etc.

5. polite •   • e. to find the answer to the problem

6. structure •   • f. someone in a position of authority in the army or government

7. solve •   • g. in the middle of something

8. officer •   • h. to help two people meet each other

B **Choose and write the correct words for the blanks.**

rich	express	peace	select	message	life

1. communicate = _____

2. death ≠ _____

3. note = _____

4. war ≠ _____

5. poor ≠ _____

6. pick = _____

C **Circle the words that best fit the sentences.**

1. We will visit the government | mall to do some shopping.

2. Main Street is the city's central | polite road.

3. The service | peace at the hotel is very good.

4. You should speak quietly in the temple | message .

5. Please express | introduce your parents to me.

6. Scientists are trying to solve | move the mysteries of the human body.

D **Choose the correct words to complete the sentences.**

1. They will _____ the winner in a few minutes.

   a. solve   b. announce   c. move   d. express

2. Mr. Peters is the head of the city _____.

   a. gate   b. peace   c. government   d. message

3. In today's _____, many people live in big cities.

   a. society   b. mall   c. officer   d. structure

4. Countries in the Middle East became _____ because of oil.

   a. peace   b. polite   c. rich   d. service

5. Look at the menu and _____ some food.

   a. solve   b. express   c. move   d. select

E **Read the passage. Then, write T for true or F for false.**

The people in Pleasantville have a nice **society**. Most people are **polite** to one another. The **government** is helpful and **solves** problems. **Life** is good there.

In Pleasantville, people can **express** their own opinions freely. They share many things. And **rich** people help the poor. The **government** provides good **services** to the people. For example, people can take a bus for free. It goes from the **central** part of the city to the countryside. There are beautiful **structures** in the city, too. There are shopping **malls**, **temples**, and museums. The police **officers** in the city help keep the **peace**.

Lots of people want to **move** to Pleasantville. But they need to be good citizens when they live there. Then, their **lives** will be great.

1. The people in Pleasantville are polite. _____

2. Rich people do not share things in Pleasantville. _____

3. There is a free bus from the city to the countryside. _____

4. People cannot have great lives in Pleasantville. _____

1	**camp** [kæmp]	*n.* a place where people sleep in tents outdoors *v.* to sleep outdoors in a tent 　set up a camp → It took one hour to set up a **camp**. 　go camping → We will go **camping** this Saturday.	
2	**exciting** [iksáitiŋ]	*adj.* making you feel very happy or interested　(ant) boring 　exciting game 　→ We had fun watching the **exciting** game.	
3	**explore** [iksplɔ́:r] *n.* explorer	*v.* to travel around a place to learn about it 　explore the ocean 　→ We need to **explore** the ocean for the future.	
4	**funny** [fʌ́ni] *n.* fun	*adj.* making you laugh　(syn) humorous 　funny story 　→ I'll tell you a **funny** story.	
5	**golden** [góuldən]	*adj.* bright yellow in color like gold 　golden sun 　→ The **golden** sun is shining brightly today.	
6	**grow** [grou] grow - grew - grown	*v.* to become bigger or older; to take care of plants　(syn) raise 　grow up → She **grew** up in a small town. 　grow rice → The farmer **grows** rice in his fields.	
7	**island** [áilənd]	*n.* land with water all around it 　desert island 　→ Nobody lives on the desert **island**.	
8	**last** [læst]	*adj.* happening or coming after all the others　(syn) final　(ant) first 　last bus 　→ When is the **last** bus to your home?	
9	**layer** [léiər]	*n.* a level of something on top of another 　thin layer 　→ There is a thin **layer** of ice on the ground.	
10	**matter** [mǽtər]	*n.* something one is discussing; the material everything is made of 　important matter → I have an important **matter** to talk about. 　properties of matter → Let's study the properties of **matter**.	

144

11 melt
[melt]

v. to change from a solid to a liquid   (ant) freeze
start to melt
→ Spring comes, and snow starts to **melt**.

12 recently
[ríːsəntli]

adv. not long ago in the past
recently receive
→ I **recently** received an email from him.

13 rice
[rais]

n. white or brown grain grown in Asia as food
eat rice
→ Many Asian people eat **rice** during meals.

14 seed
[siːd]

n. the part of a plant that can grow into a new plant
plant a seed
→ Farmers plant tomatoes **seeds** in early spring.

15 sick
[sik]

adj. not feeling well because of an illness   (syn) ill   (ant) healthy
feel sick
→ Mark felt **sick** after eating some bad food.

16 simple
[símpl]
adv. simply

adj. easy to do or understand   (ant) difficult
simple explanation
→ Her **simple** explanation was easy to understand.

17 space
[speis]

n. an empty or available area; all the area beyond the Earth   (syn) blank
take up space → This table takes up too much **space**.
travel in space → I hope to travel in **space** one day.

18 stream
[striːm]

n. a small narrow river
by a stream
→ Let's get some rest by the **stream**.

19 surface
[sə́ːrfis]

n. the top part of something
flat surface
→ People believed that the Earth had a flat **surface**.

20 valley
[væli]

n. a low area between two hills or mountains
deep valley
→ The sun set early in the **deep** valley.

A **Circle the correct definitions for the given words.**

1. explore

    a. to travel around a place to learn about it   b. to sleep outdoors in a tent

    c. to become bigger or older   d. to change from a solid to a liquid

2. layer

    a. land with water all around it   b. an empty or available area

    c. a level of something on top of another   d. a small narrow river

3. simple

    a. making you laugh   b. easy to do or understand

    c. not feeling well because of an illness   d. bright yellow in color like gold

4. matter

    a. all the area beyond the Earth   b. a low area between two hills or mountains

    c. the top part of something   d. something one is discussing

B **Write S for synonym or A for antonym next to each pair of words.**

1. _____ exciting – boring   **2.** _____ funny – humorous

3. _____ grow – raise   **4.** _____ last – first

5. _____ melt – freeze   **6.** _____ space – blank

C **Circle the words that best fit the sentences.**

1. They set up their camp | island near a big river.

2. The wheat on the farm has a golden | last color.

3. Stuart recently | simple moved to a new home.

4. Many farmers in Asia grow layer | rice in fields.

5. Few men have walked on the surface | seed of the moon.

6. We went hiking in the matter | valley last weekend.

D **Choose the correct words to complete the sentences.**

1. There are many _____ countries in the Pacific Ocean.

    a. camp   b. valley   c. surface   d. island

2. The ice _____ when the weather got warm.

    a. explored   b. melted   c. grew   d. camped

3. After planting the _____, new flowers will come up.

    a. streams   b. spaces   c. seeds   d. layers

4. I was _____ and stayed in bed for a week.

    a. simple   b. sick   c. funny   d. exciting

5. There are all kinds of fish in that _____.

    a. stream   b. layer   c. rice   d. space

E **Read the passage. Then, fill in the blanks.**

Recently, people have become interested in **exploring** new places. They do not want to visit common places anymore. Instead, they want to visit new and **exciting** places.

Some people want to visit tropical **islands**. They enjoy the **golden** sun and snorkeling in the ocean. They love walking on the beach, too. Other people want to go **camping** in a forest or **valley**. They usually set up their **camp** by a **stream**. Then, they can fish in it. They can **explore** around the **camp** site, too.

Others even want to visit **space**. They want to walk on the moon's **surface**. It can be an **exciting** experience. But trips to **space** are not common and expensive. It is the **last** place people can **explore**.

1. People want to _____ new and exciting places.

2. Some people walk on the beach on tropical _____.

3. Some people camp by a _____ and then fish in it.

4. Other people want to visit the moon and walk on its _____.

147

A   Choose and write the correct words for the definitions.

| strike | spill | sore | search |
| announce | exciting | message | sick |

1. making you feel very happy or interested ➡ _____

2. to hit something hard ➡ _____

3. having pain in one's body ➡ _____

4. to look for something ➡ _____

5. not feeling well because of an illness ➡ _____

6. to pour a liquid out of a container by accident ➡ _____

7. information given to another person ➡ _____

8. to make a public statement about a plan or decision ➡ _____

B   Circle the words that are the most similar to the underlined words.

1. The room is so <u>noisy</u> that we cannot have a conversation.
   a. comic   b. mean   c. correct   d. loud

2. The <u>wealthy</u> man purchased a large house in the countryside.
   a. simple   b. central   c. rich   d. polite

3. He wrote his name in the <u>blank</u> on the page.
   a. camp   b. space   c. matter   d. surface

4. Please try to <u>repair</u> this broken watch.
   a. pay   b. fix   c. trade   d. save

5. You will go to <u>prison</u> if you steal a car.
   a. jail   b. trip   c. excuse   d. thief

C Choose the correct forms of the words to complete the sentences.

1. That actress is really talent | talented .

2. Many explore | explorers were searching for gold and silver.

3. You need to introduce | introduction yourself in the first class.

4. Chris had the good fortune | fortunately to win the lottery.

5. He was tire | tired from playing sports all day.

D Complete the sentences with the words in the box.

1. Try not to _____ a hole in your jacket.

2. Don't _____ stones into the fish pond.

3. Her family will go on vacation to an _____.

4. Let's _____ salt together with some water.

5. There is a _____ in the middle of the wall.

island

mix

tear

gate

throw

E Write the correct phrases in the blanks.

| instead of | makes an excuse | yell at |
| computer skills | make peace | start to melt |

1. Ice will _____ outside the freezer.

2. Programmers must have very good _____.

3. He always _____ when he is late.

4. I want to read a book _____ watching a movie.

5. The two countries will _____ and stop fighting.

6. Do not _____ your friends like that.

F **Circle the mistakes. Then, write the correct sentences.**

1. I have scientific class after lunchtime.

➡ _____

2. Public serve is an important part of government work.

➡ _____

3. The cheetah is a very quickly animal.

➡ _____

4. She did very well on her finally exams.

➡ _____

5. Do you have a simply explanation for the problem?

➡ _____

G **Complete the crossword puzzle.**

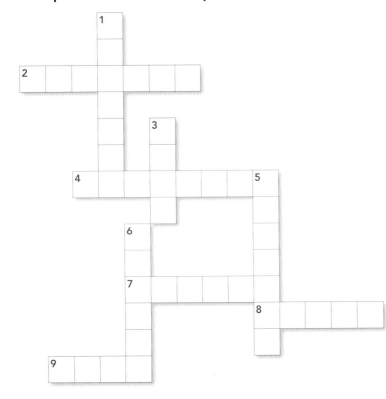

Across

2. to make something right

4. very unpleasant

7. a period of time lasting sixty seconds

8. the ability to do something well

9. white or brown grain grown in Asia as food

Down

1. a large amount of money

3. to heat something to make it catch on fire

5. to speak or write about a feeling or idea

6. a building used for the worship of a god or gods

H Read the passage. Then, answer the questions below.

Lost on an Island

 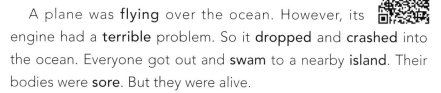

A plane was **flying** over the ocean. However, its engine had a **terrible** problem. So it **dropped** and **crashed** into the ocean. Everyone got out and **swam** to a nearby **island**. Their bodies were **sore**. But they were alive.

The next day, everyone got **busy**. They wanted to get **saved**. Some people started to **explore** the **island**. They were **searching** for food and water. Others began to make a **camp**. They built some **simple** huts.

Some people had many **talents**. So they could hunt and fish for food. They lived in **peace** on the **island** for a few weeks. Then, one day, they heard a **loud** noise. There was a plane above them. They looked up and **yelled**. They were **saved**. It was time to go home.

1. What is the passage mainly about?

   a. a fun island

   b. life after a plane crash

   c. a flight home

   d. camping on an island

2. What did the people on the island NOT do?

   a. search for food and water   b. make simple huts

   c. swim to another island   d. make a camp

3. What were the people saved by?

   a. a plane   b. a ship

   c. a helicopter   d. a train

4. Why did the plane crash?

   ➡ _____

5. How did the people live on the island?

   ➡ _____

Index

Index

Index

Index

Memo